Kid-Tastic
Birthday Parties

W9-AUK-254

OOKS ... *for living life well!*

The Complete Party Planner
for Today's Kids

PRINTED IN UNITED STATES OF AMERICA

JANE CHASE

It's so full of ideas, even if you only use a few, you'll have a great party.

—Marlys Verthein
mother of three

For the busy mother who doesn't have time to be creative, it's wonderful. All the ideas are there.

—Rachel Morgan
mother of two
city clerk

It's so easy to read, anyone who picks it up won't be able to put it down. I wish I had this book twenty years ago.

—Irene Manning
mother of six
grandmother of eleven

It's wonderful. Very age appropriate.

—Nora Vee
mother of two
administrative assistant

BRIGHTON PUBLICATIONS, INC.

Copyright © 1995 by Jane Chase

Brighton Publications, Inc.
P.O. Box 120706
St. Paul, MN 55112-0706
612-636-2220

First Edition: 1995

Library of Congress Cataloging-in-Publication Data

Chase, Jane
    Kid-tastic birthday parties : the complete party planner for today's kids / Jane Chase. — 1st ed.
        p.   cm.
    Includes index.
    1. Children's parties. 2. Birthdays. I. Title.
GV1205.C47   1995   95-2014
793.2'1—dc20   CIP
                    ISBN 0-918420-24-5

Printed in the United States of America

In memory of Wendy,
who taught children the wonders of God's world.

CONTENTS

INTRODUCTION

Making Birthday Dreams Come True

Does your child have a birthday coming up? Do you remember last year's resolve that the next party would be different? It would have eye-catching decorations kids really enjoy, great games kids truly like, and imaginative party food they actually eat. Well, here's your chance to create a theme party guaranteed to leave the kids begging for more.

The key to creating a fun party is to fill it with kids' favorite things. Youngsters love to draw, paint, glue, sculpt—anything that lets them say, "Look what I made." Pretending and role-playing have broad appeal, too. Theme parties like those in this book let children step into a fantasy land that inspires do-it-yourself fun. Even the menu suggestions add to the excitement with theme related snacks, entrees, and cakes.

Your child will want to be involved in choosing the party theme and getting ready for the party. Together, you can make decorations, choose favorite menu items, and personalize the invitations, scribbles and all. Remember, this is not the time for high expectations.

To keep your party easy to handle, limit the number of friends your child invites. A good rule of thumb is that the number of guests shouldn't be greater than the child's age. Of course, this is only a guide. If your three-year-old has four friends she *has* to invite, go ahead and break the rule. And it's best not to have your child hand out invitations at school. This way friends not invited won't feel left out.

A party doesn't have to be long to be fun. Plan on an hour and a half or two hours if you're including a full meal. Though many factors affect the length of your party, such as the number of children, the parties in this book will generally fit into two hours. This includes time to eat and open gifts.

One way you can make sure the party gets off to a good start is to do all you can so your guests will find your house easily. If your child invites friends from another neighborhood, write out directions and slip them in with the invitations. Or draw a map of where you live and run off a few copies. You don't want any guests to miss the party because they spent an hour driving around saying, "Maybe it's *this* way."

Balloons tied to the mail box or a birthday sign on your lawn will tell parents that they have found the right place.

If you can, "hire" an assistant to attend your party. It can be a spouse, friend, or older child—anyone who can squeeze a couple of hours of fun into their day, and doesn't mind being "paid" with cake, prizes, and party favors!

Your assistant's primary duty is to keep the children happy while the guests arrive and as they leave. When the party starts, you will be busy greeting parents, reminding them when to pick up their children, and ushering the guests inside. You need the assistant to get the party started with an activity others can join as they arrive. The first activity in each party is your "early bird event." It's a simple project your assistant can use to entertain the first arrivals.

During the party your assistant can help pick up balloon pieces and keep other choking hazards like popcorn kernels, peanuts, and coins out of small mouths.

Once the party is over, and the parents come to pick up their full and happy children, your assistant can keep the others occupied by reading a story or showing a video. Just make sure the wrap-up activity is a relaxing one. Parents will appreciate being able to bring home a child who's content and calm.

If you have an exceptionally wonderful assistant, she can come early to help decorate and stay afterwards to help clean up. Your assistant should be like the bread of a sandwich—visible at the beginning and end of the party, holding the meat of the party together.

Every chapter in this book highlights one party theme, complete with invitations, decorations, activities, games, menu ideas, and not one but two birthday cakes. Along with the first "early bird event," each chapter has a second craft project in the middle of the games, to give the children a rest and chance to calm down.

There are enough games in each chapter so you can pick and choose the ones your child will like best. Younger children, especially two- and three-year-olds, don't have the attention span needed for some of the games. But for this group, one game will be all you need, along with one activity, and birthday food.

Choosing teams for party games can be as fun as playing the games themselves. Many times, if you let the children choose their own teams, they will pick their friends first, or the biggest, fastest, or most popular children. You can ensure party fun for everyone by suggesting simple, non-hurtful games to choose teams or game partners. Here are a few examples.

The easiest way to choose teams is to have the children number off. To do this, point to the first child, who says, "One." The second child you point to says, "Two." Point to each child until every child is either a "one" or a "two." Then all the "ones" are on one team, and all the "twos" on the other.

This method is good because it gives the children the illusion of random team formation though you are actually in control when you point to each child.

For team selection that is truly random, let the children draw objects from a hat. To create two teams, use objects of two different colors, like red and blue marbles, black and white socks, or green and red crayons. Any objects that feel the same will work. To make three or more teams, use three or more different colored objects in the hat. Just make sure there are the same number of items as children and equal numbers of each color item so the teams will be even.

To make team selection more of a game, hide playing cards around the room before the guests arrive. Hide one card for each child. For two teams, hide half red cards and half black cards. The children search for the cards until everyone has found one. Those with red cards are on one team, and those with black cards are on the other team. You can also create four teams with cards. All the diamond cards represent one team, all the hearts another, the clubs a third, and the spades a fourth.

The children can search for other objects, too. Hide two kinds of seashells, small candies, or inexpensive favors. Anything that can be divided into two or more types will work.

In all your games, especially those for the younger children, award prizes as evenly as possible. By the end of the party, make sure every child has the same number of prizes. An armful of small prizes is more fun than one big, expensive toy. It's easier on your budget and more exciting for the children.

Part one of this book focuses on your child's special first birthday. Part two has theme suggestions for two-to five-year-olds, with the first themes best for the youngest children. This doesn't mean every game in the first chapter will be perfect for your two-year-old. Choose the games which fit your child's level of development.

This is true of parts three and four as well. Feel free to adapt the games which fit your child's level of development to the theme.

The theme-driven menus give your party the finishing touch. You might want to use all the items from a certain theme menu, or pick out one or two. Either way, feel free to add your child's favorite foods to the birthday feast.

Each chapter also includes two suggestions for a themed birthday cake—one simple cake and one for more adventurous bakers. If you're not adventurous and one of the more complicated cakes strikes your fancy, you don't have to do it yourself. Bring the idea to a local baker or cake decorating shop. Most bakers welcome the opportunity to try something new and please their customers. Give them a chance to show off their stuff!

This book will give you plenty of ideas for complete theme parties. So pick your child's favorite topic, hero, or hobby, and have fun with it. Use one of the themes in this book, or let a theme spark your imagination and do your own thing. A homemade birthday party is like homemade ice cream—truly high quality. It will make your child's birthday party a dream come true.

PART ONE

The First Birthday Stands Alone

A traditional birthday party is filled with games, laughter, and birthday cake. However, your child's first birthday is a different event altogether. At one year old, your child won't be playing Pin the Tail on the Donkey, running relay races, or blowing out birthday candles. So how do you celebrate an infant's birthday? You create a special day that stands alone!

A Birthday to Cherish

Do you remember your first birthday? Most people don't. But most people do remember their child's first birthday. Make your child's special day one everyone will cherish with memories that won't fade with time.

Record the Day

One way to preserve that day is by making a record of all it contains. Begin first thing in the morning, by reading the daily paper. That might not sound like an interesting way to start your child's first birthday, but it will get your record keeping off to a running start.

Take note of the important headlines, including politics, economic news, and entertainment. Record the high and low temperatures for the day, and whether it was sunny, windy, or snowing.

Then put aside the paper and note other tidbits that are more personal, such as whether the first strawberries became ripe enough to pick that day, or if you found rabbit tracks in the deep snow in your backyard.

Remember the Relatives

And don't forget the relatives. Record how events in their lives fit in with your child's birthday. For example, Tommy turned one the same day cousin Sally graduated from high school. Or, Martha was six weeks pregnant with Jill on Tommy's first birthday. Friends and relatives will be thrilled to be a part of your child's history.

You can record anything in your world that captures your fancy. Then, type up the information and run off a few copies, or take it to a printer for a more professional look. Set it aside for now.

Record Your Child

Next, get personal. It's your child's day, so record your child. Get a piece of paper and trace around his hands and feet. Years later, it will be hard to believe he was ever that small. Write other personal facts on the page, too. For example, your child crawls like a maniac, has begun to walk, or knows how to say "Dada." Write down physical characteristics that are unusual or unique to your family. One day your child will be able to look back and see how characteristics were prominent even at one year old.

When the physical record is complete, add this page to the history page. Staple or clip them together and give them to close friends and relatives. But make sure to file away at least one copy for safekeeping. In following years, you can add to the record—a history page and a personal page for each year. Your child's record of life will bring back precious memories for years to come.

Start a Collection

To get your child involved in the record of life, begin a tradition he can be part of. Start a collection of seashells, stamps, ceramic animals, or Christmas ornaments. People's most cherished collections are often those that are started when they are young. As your child grows, he can build the collection on his own. Imagine being forty or fifty years old and having a collection that began when you were one!

Better yet, plant a tree for your child on his birthday. As he and the tree grow together, teach him to take care of it. When a child learns to nourish living things, he develops a sense of responsibility and compassion that will grow in him.

Keep the Party Simple

When it's time for the birthday party, remember to keep it simple. It's tempting to invite everyone you know to this great event, but hold back. Too many people will just upset your child and turn the day into one you'd rather not remember.

A Long Distance Birthday

For those who can't be with you, deliver a long-distance birthday. If you don't have a video camera, borrow or rent one and make your own birthday movie. Make sure not to miss the highlights—eating cake and opening presents. And zoom in when your child opens gifts sent by those who will receive the video. They'll love seeing your child's reaction to the gift they picked out.

Video and Audio Records

And you don't have to limit your video to specific birthday activities. Take your child outside and record his curious exploration of the grass and flowers, or the beetle crawling across the sidewalk. In the winter, record his reaction to falling snow and sparkling icicles.

But don't get so busy running the tape that you forget to interact with your child. When he giggles, giggle with him. Encourage him with conversation and your own enthusiasm. Give your viewers a show they'll love.

This isn't the best time to record your child's "firsts," like his first meeting with the neighbor's collie. Firsts can be wonderful, but can also be frightfully unpredictable. If the collie sends your child into uncontrollable tears, the festive mood of your video will be quite ruined.

It's better, and safer, to record accomplished behaviors. Show off how many words your child can say (even if you have to "interpret" some of them). Demonstrate how well he cooperates when you dress him, and how he is only "days away" from being able to stack blocks.

Don't worry if you accidentally film the basket of laundry sitting in the corner, or the cat walking by in the background. Years later, that cat will spark more memories of your day, and you might even get nostalgic about the clothes you recognize in the basket.

If you don't have access to a video camera, or the people who would receive the tape don't have a VCR, an audio tape is the next best thing. Observe carefully and describe all that your child does. With vivid descriptions, your listeners will see the birthday in their minds.

Record any words your child knows, and any other vocalization. Relatives, especially grandparents, love listening to baby talk, including gurgles, giggles, and babbles. To bring your listeners even closer, have a recording of the song, "It's a Small World" playing in the background as your child talks.

A Care Package

When you send your video or audio tape, include a complete care package. Send a card with your child's handprint and "signature." Scrawled crayon lines "written" by your child mean more to relatives than the most famous autograph. Also include copies of your compiled historical and personal records.

Finish off the care package with samples of your day. A leaf from your child's tree, a block from his new building set, or a birthday napkin are all good keepsakes. You can even send a small piece of cake. If you zip it in a sandwich bag, and pack it in a box with styrofoam packing pieces, it will arrive in good shape.

The Birthday "Cake"

Speaking of cakes, here's something to keep in mind. A birthday cake with lots of icing and a single candle is traditional, but you might not want to feed your child all that sugar. Instead, serve banana bread baked in a round cake pan, or a cake-shaped jello filled with fruit. At a year old, your child won't know what he's missing, and most adults will find it a refreshing change.

Be Flexible

Probably the most important aspect of your child's first birthday is flexibility. Everyone has bad days. If your child is having one on his birthday, don't try to make him smile for the camera. You can still record what the day is like and major news events, both public and personal, but the party can wait.

Years later, it won't matter if you postponed the party for a day or two, or if your child opened presents in the afternoon instead of before lunch. It's more important to have a birthday that's happy than a birthday that's at 2:00 P.M. on Tuesday.

Your child's first birthday is the first of many for him. As one birthday follows another, he will forget that first one. But you won't. Do all you can to hold that memory, to capture life at its most precious.

PART TWO

Themes to Thrill the Younger Ones

From two to five years of age, children develop a variety of interests and skills that can be woven into party activities. Two- and three-year-olds aren't ready for a highly structured party, but they will enjoy an arrival activity and one game.

Games and activities in the first chapters in this section are suited more for the two- and three-year-olds, while the later chapters have more games suitable for four- and five-year-olds. But this doesn't mean every game in the first chapters will be perfect for your two-year-old. Games like Hungary Elephant, Super Feats III, and Triceratops Toss can be adapted for the younger children.

When planning a party for two- and three-year-olds, you will want to invite the guests' parents as well. With fewer children and more adults, you will have plenty of supervision for each child.

Once children are four to five, they have distinct memories of parties and more patience for organization. They are now ready for a traditional party with all the activities your sanity and time will allow. The themes in this section provide a wealth of possibilities for this age child.

But no matter how old your guests are, remember that every child should go home with the same number of prizes. Youngsters are easily hurt, and even the best theme party can't make up for wounded feelings. So relax with your favorite beverage and look through these themes for the two-to-five crowd.

Step Right Up and See the Show!

The circus is coming to town! Bring the circus right into your living room with a party chock full of clowns, caramel corn, and all the fun of the big top.

Clown and Balloon Invitations

Kids can't resist clowns, so let your child create a cheerful clown invitation for each guest. Using the illustration as a guide, draw clowns for your child to color, then fill in the party information with a black pen or fine point marker (fig. 1). If your toddler's coloring consists of scribbles, let him or her color on the back, while you take over the front.

For an invitation that will "blow" their minds, blow up a balloon and write the invitation with a permanent marker. While the balloon is inflated, you'll be able to write on it easily. Then let the air out. The words will shrink so your guests will have to blow it up again to read the invitation. Slip the balloon in an envelope with the instructions, "Blow me up for a chance to see the greatest

fig. 1

show on earth!" With this invitation, the guests already have a party favor before even coming to the party!

Welcome to the Big Top

Welcome the guests to your circus with a sign on the front door saying, "Welcome to the Big Top!" Cut it in the shape of a tent and use bright red, yellow, and blue markers to make it stand out (fig. 2).

fig. 2

Inside, give your living room a "big top" look by draping crepe paper streamers from the middle of the ceiling to the walls. The more streamers you use, the greater "tent effect" you will achieve. The traditional circus tent is red and white, so make tent stripes by alternating a few red streamers, then a few white ones, to create wide panels of color.

That "Circus" Look

Clowns are the highlight of the circus act, so fill your big top with colorful clown heads made from balloons and construction paper.

To do this, first blow up a balloon and tie the mouth closed with a long piece of string. Make a hat from a piece of construction paper rolled into a cone and taped together. Take the end of the balloon's string and push it through the hole in the top of the paper cone. Go in the wide end and out the pointed tip. When you pull the string all the way through, it will pull the balloon up to the open end of the cone, so it looks like a hat.

fig. 3

Tie a yarn pom-pom to the hat's tip. Then draw a clown face and decorations with markers. Curly ribbon or streamers taped to the bottom of the balloon will finish it off. Tack the end of the string to the ceiling (fig. 3).

Make your own yarn pom-poms by wrapping yarn around and around a square of cardboard. Cut the yarn off the cardboard, then cut the bundle of pieces again for a deeper, thicker pile (fig. 4). Tie a string tightly around the middle of the pieces. If you tie it tightly enough, the yarn pieces will stick out in every direction, forming a ball. Trim uneven ends.

fig. 4

A circus isn't complete without wild animals, jugglers, and acrobats. So make posters of elephants, lions, and circus acts with ideas from coloring books or children's picture books. What's that? You say you're not good at drawing? Your posters don't have to be elaborate. Simple pictures of top hats, juggling pins, and clown faces will give your tent a convincing "circus" atmosphere.

Joining the Circus

And what could be more fun than watching a circus? Being in the circus! As the children arrive, let them all join the circus by making their own clown hats.

Staple construction paper cones beforehand, and let the children decorate them with markers and adhesive stickers. Even two-year-olds can scribble designs on hats. Punch holes at opposite sides of the hat and strengthen them with adhesive hole reinforcements. Tie on an elastic string to slip under the child's chin. Cord elastic comes in black and white and can be purchased at hobby or fabric stores. Now the clowns are ready for the show.

Rolling Clowns

Before the party, use paint or permanent markers to make colorful clown faces on lemons—enough so there's one lemon for each child. Hand out the clown lemons and pencils for everyone. The children must get on their hands and knees and use the pencils to push the lemons across the floor. For the youngest children, skip the pencils. Crawling and rolling lemons with their hands is enough of a challenge. The first one to get her lemon across the finish line is the top clown. Let them all keep their lemon clowns, and give the top clown an extra prize.

Hungry Elephant

Since elephants eat a quarter of a ton of food each day, they always seem hungry. Especially circus elephants, who work up an appetite performing all those tricks. Let your guests "feed" the circus elephant by tossing peanuts into its trunk.

First, make one or more hungry elephants. Start by making a cone out of gray construction paper, leaving the point of the cone slightly open. Tape a cardboard roll from toilet tissue or paper towels to the cone's point to form the elephant's trunk. Cut out large ears from gray paper and tape them to the top of the cone. Finally, draw eyes and trunk wrinkles (fig. 5). Pin the elephant to window curtains or tape it to a wall. Then place a bowl on the floor under the trunk to catch the peanuts as they fall through.

fig. 5

Your clown guests must stand in a line to toss peanuts into the elephant's trunk. They get a small prize for every peanut that lands in the trunk. For a game of mutual encouragement and cooperation, let them work in teams to feed the elephant, and award one larger prize to each member of the winning team.

Since two-year-olds are fascinated by filling and emptying things, they'll enjoy filling the elephant without points or competition. To make it easier for these young folks, you may have them just run up and place the peanuts into the trunk instead of tossing them.

Three Ring Circus

If the children have a wide range of physical skills, play the Three Ring Circus, a target game that gives everyone an equal chance.

Fill a bucket with water, and stand a large jar in the water, so it is completely submerged. Stand a smaller jar inside the larger one, to create three "rings." Children must drop pennies into the bucket of water, aiming for the center ring. The largest ring is worth one point, the middle ring worth three, and the smallest ring worth five. Highest point total wins. Of course, no matter how well the children aim, the pennies zig-zag and swirl through the water! For the youngest children, the movement of the coins will intrigue them without any need to keep score.

During this game, make sure to watch the children closely so they don't pop the pennies in their mouths. This is a greater danger for the youngest children, but for this age most likely there will be other parents around to help supervise.

When it's time for the intermission between shows, let the children make circus lion puppets. Prepare ahead by gluing tongue depressors to paper plates. The children can make them into lions by drawing faces and gluing on construction paper ears and yarn manes.

The best glue for this is the glue sticks sold in discount and craft stores. They are inexpensive and easy to use. For children who can handle glue bottles, buy several of the small 1.25-ounce ones found in craft and discount stores. You don't have to purchase one for each child, but enough so they can share easily. Some stores also carry assorted colored glues, besides the traditional white.

fig. 6

Of course, two-year-olds won't be able to draw faces, but they can draw scribbles and pretend they are lion faces. Help the young ones glue, and cut out the eyes to make masks (fig. 6).

Lion Tamer

After making lion masks, it's time to tame the lions. Arrange chairs in a circle with the chairs facing inward, one chair fewer than the number of children. One child is the lion tamer, who stands in the middle of the circle of chairs. The rest of the children are lions, and each sits in a chair.

Two-year-olds can play this if the lion tamer is an older child or an adult. Toddlers love to run and play imaginary games, so even the youngest ones can have fun with "Lion Tamer."

The lion tamer walks around in the circle and says, "I'm the circus lion tamer and I've tamed Sarah the lion." Sarah gets up and follows the lion tamer. The lion tamer says, "I'm the circus lion tamer and I've tamed Tommy the lion." Tommy follows the lion tamer and Sarah. When several lions have been tamed, the lion tamer says, "Oh, no, the lions are wild!" The children who have been following the lion tamer race to the empty chairs. The lion who doesn't get a chair becomes the lion tamer.

Give prizes to all the lions who are well-trained. And of course, *all* the lions in *this* circus are well trained!

Circus Tower

Circus performers must climb high towers to reach the high trapeze. It's up to the circus crew to build those high towers.

Divide the children into teams and see who can build the highest tower out of paper cups. Colored party cups will add a festive flair to the stacking, and they'll create an explosion of color when they tumble down. Two- and three-year-olds may have trouble with cups, so use colorful wooden blocks instead.

Award prizes for the highest tower, for creativity, cooperation, and sportsmanship. In the circus, everyone works together to make a spectacular show!

Clown Pizza

One of the best parts of going to a circus is eating fun food. Make circus food with clown pizza, carousel cupcakes, and clown cones.

Start with a large cheese pizza, and add your own clown face. Before baking, sprinkle bits of chopped tomato along the top edge of the pizza to make clown hair. Use slices of pepperoni for the eyes and nose. Make the mouth by cutting a slice lengthwise off a polish sausage. This long, curved piece makes a smiling mouth.

Clown Ice Cream

Continue the clown theme with ice cream clowns you can make ahead. Flatten a paper baking cup on a saucer and place a large scoop of ice cream in the center of the flat paper. Use colored chocolate candies to make eyes and the nose, and use licorice for the mouth. Press colored coconut into the ice cream for hair. You can make white shredded coconut any color you want by putting some coconut in a plastic bag with a few drops of food coloring. Shake the bag until the coconut is evenly coated. Make a clown hat with a pointed sugar cone, and push a cherry onto the tip (fig. 7).

fig. 7

Carousels, Big and Small

It's easy to make carousel cupcakes by poking a miniature umbrella into each frosted cupcake. Iced animal crackers prancing under the umbrella complete the carousel. You can also use zoo animal fruit snacks or animal cookies.

For a grand carousel, make one out of the birthday cake. Prepare and frost a round layer cake according to package directions. Press licorice whips onto the sides of the cake for carousel poles. But first cut each piece of licorice in half, and leave a space between the two pieces when you put them on the cake. Press an animal cracker into the space so it looks like the pole is going right through the animal. Sprinkle candy decorettes on top of the cake for a festive look (fig. 8).

fig. 8

Another Birthday Cake

You can also turn an ordinary round cake into a circus clown. Bake and frost as usual, then create a fun clown face using colored coconut for hair, round orange or lemon slices for eyes, a cherry nose, and a licorice mouth. If you have a flair for decorating with icing, use decorator icing tubes to draw a clown face like the ones on your invitations, or like the balloon clowns hanging from the ceiling.

Party Favors

Children will go home from the circus with plenty of favors. Besides their masks, puppets, and clown hats, give away the posters and clown balloons from the big top. Boxes of circus animal crackers and plastic circus animals are good prizes, too.

Fun Food

You can also award fun circus food like popcorn, caramel corn, and candy circus peanuts. Give other kinds of nuts like honey roasted peanuts, burnt peanuts, and mixed nuts.

If you can spend a little more money, rent a helium machine and make your own helium-filled balloons. You or your assistant can be a balloon seller, and the balloons only cost peanuts—literally!

Circus Prizes

With small packs of theater makeup, sets of markers, and crayons for prizes, your guests can make their own circus fun at home.

When the circus ends, every child will go home with delightful memories of the party that was the greatest show on earth!

3

Hero for a Day

Bam! Pow! Smash! Batman saves the day again! Or Superman or Spiderman or Wonder Woman. Your child's favorite superheroes make a great theme for a birthday party. The dynamic action and bright colors will thrill your child and his guests.

Eye-catching Invites

First, invitations. For a superhero to keep his identity a secret, he must wear a mask. So send mask invitations to the guests. Cut out masks from poster board following the patterns provided (fig. 1). Punch holes in the sides and strengthen them with plastic adhesive

fig. 1

hole reinforcements. Tie on cord elastic.

Then write party information on the inside of the mask, and invite your guests to wear their masks to the party. Only superheroes are allowed at this party!

fig. 1

You can also make invitations using superhero symbols. Cut out a Superman shield, but replace the "S" with your child's first initial (fig. 2). This way the guests will instantly know how "super" your child is.

fig. 2

Use the same pattern, but larger, to make a poster to hang on your front door. Cut it out of tagboard and paint it red and yellow.

A Superhero's Hideaway

Inside decorations are a job for Super Party Planner! Turn your house into a superhero's hideaway with "S" emblems, lightning bolts, and star bursts with words like "Thwaack," "Bam," and "Zoom" in the centers (fig. 3). Cut them out of colored construction paper, or use white tagboard and color them with magic markers. Use bright streamers of yellow, red, and blue to carry the superheroes color scheme. If your child has posters of favorite heroes hanging in his room, see if you can borrow them for the party.

fig. 3

A Super Table

Keep the theme going by using the Superman shield for place mats. Use the illustration provided (fig. 4), or replace each "S" with each child's initial. When places at the table are designated, there will be no arguments over who sits next to whom.

fig. 4

If your child collects action figures, use them to create a superhero scene in the center of your dining table. Let's say your child has a Batman figure. Stand Batman on a sidewalk made out of gray construction paper. Draw black lines to show the curb and sidewalk cracks. Turn a plain shoe box into a building by standing it on end and drawing windows and doors with a marker. Weigh it down with a rock or other object so it won't tip over.

Then, tape three fish hooks together with the points outward to look like a grappling hook. This is Batman's "bat hook." Tape one end of a string to the fish hook shanks, and place the other end in Batman's hand. Once you hook the bat hook to the top of the building, Batman is ready to swing into action!

Use like props that are easily available to create centerpiece scenes for other superheroes.

Masks and Capes

When the "superheroes" arrive for the party, some will be wearing their invitation masks, but some won't. So the first thing to do is turn everyone into a superhero. Cut out masks for those who didn't bring theirs, and let them all decorate their masks with adhesive stars, glitter, or sequins. For the youngest children, avoid a frustrating mess by limiting the decorating supplies to crayons and stickers.

But a superhero needs more than a mask. He also needs a costume, and the most important part of a costume is the cape. Cut a red, plastic disposable table cover into large squares, giving one square to each child. Let them write their names with glue and sprinkle glitter over the letters. They can also glue on lightning bolts and stars. Two- and three-year-olds can draw marker designs while you write their names.

Finish the cape by laying a piece of string along the top edge, folding the edge over the string and securing it with vinyl tape. Tie the string around the child's neck with the cape in the back. Let your superheroes run around a bit, to test out their capes, and burn off some super energy.

X-Ray Vision

To find out how powerful your superheroes really are, test their X-ray vision with a penny search. Make the search more interesting by hiding a few nickels and dimes, too. When all the coins have been found, the heroes can purchase prizes with their money, or keep the money as their reward. If there are a few coins the children can't find, you'll know it must be because the coins are hidden behind something that's lined with lead! This game is great for all ages, since even two-year-olds love to explore. Just make sure to keep an eye on those pennies. Superheroes shouldn't swallow pennies.

Super Feats

Everyone knows that Superman can leap buildings in a single bound. Test your superheroes' leaping ability with a city made of boxes. Create your city the same way you made the building for the table centerpiece. If you have time, embellish the buildings with cut-out windows and doors, painted trim, and cardboard chimneys.

Keep the box buildings small enough so your heroes can leap over them easily, whether they are two years old or five. Have the children take turns jumping over each building in sequence, or divide them into teams for a relay. Superman flies faster than a speeding bullet. See how fast your guests can leap all the buildings. The fastest hero, or team of heroes, gets the super prize!

Since every movie about superheroes has a sequel, here comes the sequel to Super feats:

Super Feats II

Superman has a habit of catching people when they fall from tall buildings. See how well your heroes do trying to catch a falling feather! While standing on a chair or other high place, reach out and drop a single feather. It will swirl and spiral all over. The heroes can take turns trying to catch it, or work in pairs. For all-out chaos, grab a handful of feathers and throw them into space at once. Award a small prize for each feather caught.

Super Feats III

The sequel to the sequel. For feats that guarantee winners all around, test abilities like walking around the room with books on their heads, touching their toes, or standing on one foot. Even superheroes enjoy the thrill of accomplishing feats that don't require all their super powers!

Superstars

Give your guests the chance to recreate superheroes in action in their own mini-movie. The birthday child gets to be his favorite superhero, while the rest of the children fill other roles. Using Superman as an example of your child's favorite hero, other children can play the parts of Lois, Jimmy, Perry White, Superman's parents, and villains. Make the plot simple, and let the actors ad-lib lines as they go.

For a Superman story, let's say Lois and Jimmy are walking down the street. Two crooks jump out and grab Lois. They try to kidnap her, but Superman saves her. Meanwhile, Jimmy takes pictures of the whole thing, and Superman's parents call out, "That's our boy!" Bystanders can cheer Superman and boo the criminals.

This game suits a variety of personalities, since the more outgoing children can have large parts, while shy ones can be bystanders.

Super Burgers

When the show is over, reward everyone for making such a wonderful superhero movie.

Your heroes will have worked up a super appetite, so feed them with a supersized super burger. Start with a round loaf of Hawaiian bread, which is sold in most grocery stores. Or, if you like to bake, make your own bread in a round cake pan.

When the loaf is cool, slice it like a gigantic hamburger bun. If you want, slice it twice to make a double hamburger.

Make a huge hamburger patty out of a full pound of ground beef. Press it together firmly, and turn it carefully so it doesn't break while cooking. Top the burger with lots of lettuce, slices of tomato, and pickles.

Serve the super burger whole on a platter, and slice it into pie-shaped pieces at the table. Let each hero add his own condiments.

Hero Sandwiches

For more traditional fare, treat your superheroes to hero sandwiches. Give each sandwich a super identity by using small decorations on picks. These can be purchased at craft and hobby stores.

For example, add a plastic bat for a Batman sandwich, a spider for a Spiderman sandwich, a fish for Aquaman, and a flag for Captain America. Or, make your own picks. A piece of popcorn dyed with green food coloring can be a piece of kryptonite. Poke a toothpick through it and stick it on a Superman sandwich. A piece of string painted yellow makes a fine lariat for a Wonder Woman sandwich. Strolling through a craft store will give you more ideas for hero sandwich decorations.

Eating all these sandwiches is sure to make your heroes thirsty, so treat them to "pow punch." Add a carbonated beverage like ginger ale to fruit juice for a sparkling fizz your guests will love.

Emblem Cake

Then, it's time for the cake.

It's easy to turn a square cake into a superhero emblem by cutting off one corner (fig. 5). Use your superhero shield invitations as a guide to ice the cake. Decorator tubes of red and yellow frosting will make this work easy.

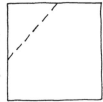

fig. 5

For a bright cake that takes less time, bake the cake as usual, then frost it with bright yellow icing and add red candy sprinkles. The red and yellow will give the cake a "super" look without your doing another thing!

Super Prizes

To round out your super party, give prizes and favors that complement your superhero theme. For small prizes, use super-blow bubble gum or toy rubber balls with a high bounce.

Excellent larger prizes are inexpensive comic books or coloring books featuring your child's favorite superheroes, along with action figures and accessories like tiny Batmobiles. Discount stores sell all kinds of small items like notebooks, pins, and hair accessories with superheroes on them. Keep your eyes open and you'll find ideas everywhere.

After spending the afternoon at a superhero party, everyone will go home feeling just "super!"

Prehistoric Place Mats

Your guests can make their own dinosaur place mats to complete the prehistoric table. Give everyone a piece of stiff paper, the size of a place mat, and let them create original pictures by tracing around odd-shaped puzzle pieces. The piece shapes turn into prehistoric monsters when the children draw eyes, claws, scales, or armored skin. The youngest children can trace around the large wooden puzzle pieces made for small hands. Give them fat crayons to draw with, and watch so they don't try to eat them. With a little imagination, even the most scribbled tracings will look like prehistoric beasts.

Children who are old enough to handle scissors can cut dinosaurs out of coloring books and glue them onto plain paper. They can finish the scene by drawing tropical plants in the background, making their dinosaurs look right at home.

When the place mats are finished, arrange them at the table where each child will sit. Just before eating, flip the pictures over, unless you have clear contact paper to cover the place mats. Clear contact paper is self-sticking plastic with removable backing, perfect for protecting these fine works of art. Look for the paper at your local discount store or hardware store.

Digging for Fossils

You have already given each child a bone "fossil" if you sent bone invitations. This game gives them a chance to become archaeologists and discover their own dinosaur bones. Scrub chicken bones and pork bones clean, then hide them around the house or yard. Give a small prize for every bone discovered, or prizes for the most bones found. And award a special prize for the archaeologist who discovers a real dinosaur egg—a watermelon! And you can eat the "egg" at lunchtime.

Triceratops Toss

In this game, the archaeologists become cave dwellers and must face a fierce triceratops.

Before the party, make the triceratops by cutting three holes in a cardboard box and inserting paper towel rolls into the holes. Tape them in

place, pointing slightly upwards. Add marker eyes.
Cut a bony neck shield out of construction paper,
and glue it to the back (fig. 3).
Give the cave dwellers rings of "dinosaur verte-
brae" made out of rings of cardboard. Award points
for each ring tossed onto a horn. Give each of the
three horns different point values, and make the   fig. 3
game more of a challenge by *subtracting* points for rings that land inside
the box. This can be a team game, or played individually. Two-year-olds will
need to stand close to the dinosaur, and won't care about points.

3-D Dinosaurs

In movies about prehistoric times, the cavemen are usually grunting,
bearded, beast-like men who show no class or creativity. Let your cave
dwellers show their creative side by making their own model dinosaurs.
The two- and three-year-olds' dinosaurs will be the most "creative" of all!

You can purchase modeling clay, or make your own clay by mixing 2 1/4
cups flour, 1 cup salt, and 4 tablespoons of oil. Stir in 1 1/2 cups of boiling
water. When the clay is cool enough to handle, knead it to a smooth consis-
tency. For an authentic dinosaur look, mix in green food color. Add a touch
of red to give the green a brownish hue. Make the clay ahead of time. It will
last a long time in the refrigerator.

For a more involved project, let the cave dwellers paint their creations
with poster paint. Encourage creative colors. Though real dinosaurs were
probably gray, green, and brown, no one said there *couldn't* be a purple
dinosaur with yellow and orange stripes!

Let the paint dry for about ten minutes, so you can handle the creations
without getting dinosaur-colored fingers. Place the dinosaurs on a baking
sheet and cook them in the oven at 225 degrees for an hour. While they're
cooking, play other games and eat lunch.

Erupting Volcanoes

Back when the earth was young and its crust was still settling and surg-
ing, volcanoes erupted constantly. Dinosaurs were often trapped and killed

in unexpected lava flows. But your four- and five-year-old cave dwellers can control this lava flow.

For this game, you will need a long piece of cardboard about a foot wide, two buckets, and a box with enough styrofoam packing peanuts to fill those two buckets. You'll also need two more containers, either cardboard boxes or more buckets.

The best place to get a big piece of cardboard is from a refrigerator shipping carton, or one of those boxes that build-it-yourself bookcases come in. Check at gift stores and department stores for styrofoam peanuts. And the most enjoyable way to get buckets is to devour 5-quart pails of ice cream!

The idea of this game is for the cave dwellers to catch the lava (peanuts) as it erupts from the volcano (box) and flows down the mountain (cardboard strip). The first team to fill their bucket wins.

The setup is simple. Divide the cave dwellers into two teams and give each team a bucket. Bend the long piece of cardboard lengthwise, so it makes a V-shaped trough. Place one end in the container on the floor. Rest the other end on a chair back. The two teams line up behind each other on either side of the mountain. Each team's bucket is behind the last person in the line (fig. 4).

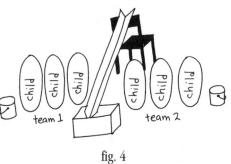

fig. 4

When the cave dwellers are in place, pour the box of styrofoam peanuts down the cardboard trough. Pour them slowly, to make a thin stream of peanuts sliding down the mountain. The first person on each team grabs a handful of peanuts as they slide by, and hands each handful to the person behind him. The peanuts are passed down the line to the last person, who drops them in the bucket.

Have your assistant standing by with an empty box. As your lava supply runs out, your assistant can shift the bottom of the mountain slope to the spare box and hand you the lava until one team has filled their bucket.

The fastest team gets the best prize, but all the cave dwellers deserve rewards after facing this dangerous lava flow.

A Real Lava Flow

After the fake lava flow, show your cave dwellers what a real volcano looks like. This demonstration takes some preparation, but the dramatic effect is worth it.

Fill a shallow cardboard box with wet sand and bury a soup can in the middle so the sand comes up to the edge of the can (fig. 5). Put 1/4 cup baking soda in the empty can. Mix together 1 cup water, 3/4 cup vinegar, and 1/2 cup dishwashing liquid. For a realistic touch, add red and yellow food color to the solution.

When it's time for the demonstration, pour the vinegar solution into the can and watch the volcano erupt! It's a good idea to cover the table with a plastic disposable cover. Volcanoes can be messy!

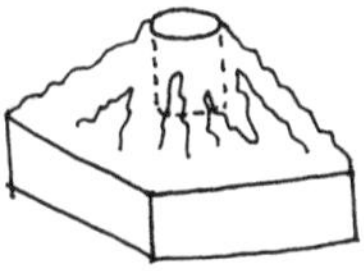

fig. 5

A Prehistoric Meal

When you're ready to eat, treat your cave dwellers to a real prehistoric meal. Back when dinosaurs roamed, danger lurked everywhere, and cave dwellers kept their weapons close at hand. Give your cave dwellers clubs in case one of the dinosaurs lurking in the foliage attacks—a club that is really a chicken leg!

Give them dinosaur eggs—extra large boiled eggs with the shells dyed green and brown. To make safe dye, just add a few drops of food color to the water when you boil the eggs. Or use Easter egg dyes, which are also nontoxic. If you crack the shells slightly before dyeing them, the color will seep inside and dye the egg itself, for a real prehistoric look. Nestle the dinosaur eggs in a nest of cooked spinach noodles.

And how can there be dinosaur eggs without dinosaurs? Make a breadstick dinosaur for each cave dweller. Start with prepared breadstick dough from the grocery store, or make your own bread dough. Cut four pieces off the end of each stick and place them along the sides of the body for legs. Pinch one end into a long tail, and press raisins into the other end for eyes (fig. 6).

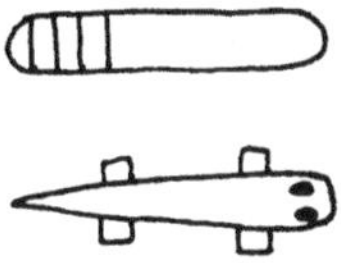

fig. 6

If you have more time and ambition, add details to your prehistoric lizard. Pull a ridge of dough up along its back, like the armored plates of

For variety, roll chocolate bananas in crushed cereal, crushed cookies, or butterscotch chips. Or, put flaked coconut into a sandwich bag, add a few drops of food coloring and shake until the coconut is evenly colored. Roll bananas in a rainbow of bright coconut colors. Use your imagination to make all kinds of magic bananas. Your guests will love these "invisible" bananas.

Make cookies to complement your magical scene with sugar cookie cutouts. Mix candy sprinkles into plain sugar cookie dough for a fun sparkle. Cut out stars, and make moons by cutting overlapping circles. For more elaborate cookies, make rabbits using a circle for the head, and two slightly straightened "moon" crescents for ears. Add chocolate chip eyes and nose. They say rabbit tastes like chicken, but these sure don't!

A "Starring" Cake

Give your child's birthday cake that magic look by stirring candy sprinkles or M&M's into the batter before baking. Once the cake is cooled and frosted, press sprinkles onto the sides of the cake and add a border of star cookies to the top. Candles between the stars and a few more sprinkles finish the creation.

Or, make a rabbit cake in just a few steps. First, bake a round cake according to the package directions. Then, cut the cake as shown (fig. 5). Cover a large platter or baking tray with tin foil. Place the cake pieces on the foil serving plate with the two side pieces as ears and the small triangle piece for a nose. Fasten pieces with icing and frost cake completely. Use red ring-

fig. 5

shaped candies for eyes and black shoelace licorice for whiskers. If desired, use red food coloring to color a small amount of white icing and frost the nose with pink. Place a row of pink candles in each ear (fig. 6). Then, watch the rabbit disappear!

fig, 6

The Magic Goes On

Prizes for your games don't need to be elaborate. It is more important to see that everyone wins something than to have extravagant prizes. Small packs of stickers are good prizes, as well as candy like magic pop-rocks, lollipops with the "surprise" center, and small chocolate or marshmallow rabbits. For larger prizes, use an assortment of inexpensive tricks from a magic store, toy store, or gift shop. You can also give out "silk" scarves or plastic toy bunnies.

If you don't plan to use a magic theme in coming years, send your decorations home with guests. Let them keep their marbleized place mats (if clean), and give them each a balloon to take home. Even your cut-out wall decorations can become party favors. If you anticipate a great demand for take-home decorations, write a number on the back of each cut-out before hanging it. Let the children guess or draw numbers to see which decorations they get to keep.

By the time the party is over, every child will feel like a real magician. Watch out for invitations to future magic shows put on by your guests!

Favorite Fairy Tale Films

Children love the animated stories of Walt Disney. Classics like *Pinocchio, 101 Dalmations,* and *Sleeping Beauty* have been joined by more recent favorites like *Aladdin, Beauty and the Beast,* and *The Lion King.* Any of these wonderful tales can be used to plan your child's birthday.

As an example, let's look at how a party can be based on *The Little Mermaid,* the story of a mermaid who loves a human.

Clam Invitations

Invitations to a mermaid party can be made on real clam shells. Hobby and craft stores sell packages of assorted sea shells, including scallop shells. The scallops look like clam shells, but have ridges and are more colorful.

Write the message on the inside of the shell with permanent marker. Use phrases that will emphasize the sea theme right from the start. "Welcome, mermaids and mermen. Life is much better, here where it's wetter, at Sally's mermaid party."

Or, use the pattern provided to make shell shapes out of stiff paper. Fold on the dotted line so the shell will open (fig. 1). Color the front with pastel lavender, pink, and peach tones to make it look like a real scallop.

Welcome
Mermaids
and
Mermen

to
- - - - - - - -
Kathy's
Little
Mermaid
Party
1220 Pearl Drive
May 14
3:00 - 5:00

fig. 1

Under the Sea

Keep the shell pattern to make large shells to hang on your walls. Also cut out fish shapes, starfish, sea horses, and crabs, using the illustrations as a guide (fig. 2). Hang blue and green streamers from the ceiling and add bunches of blue and green balloons. To give your green streamers an authentic seaweed look, fold a long piece of crepe paper several times, and crimp the edges. When you unfold it, the edges will have a fluted, ripply look.

Packages of plastic shells are inexpensive and can be purchased at hobby stores, toy stores, and often at flea markets, boutiques and garage sales. They will add to your decor when arranged on shelves and tables. If your budget allows, purchase fishnet to drape from the ceiling or on one wall. Hang shells and plastic starfish in the netting.

If you have any fishermen in the family, you will have access to all kinds of free stuff. Hang bobbers from fishing line tacked to the ceiling. Stand fishing poles in the corner and leave a

fig. 2

scoop net, a boat anchor, and bait bucket in strategic places. If you're even more ambitious, haul in boat oars and life jackets. Anything relating to fish or the sea will fit into this theme.

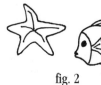

fig. 2

Your dinner table provides even more opportunities for sea-related embellishments. Fill clam shells with mints or nuts and leave one at each person's place. Cut fish-shaped place mats from large construction paper, and use flat green and blue streamers for table runners.

Watermelon Boat

Little Mermaid viewers know that Ariel falls in love with Eric the sailor when she sees him on his ship. So recreate Eric's ship with a watermelon centerpiece. Draw guidelines on the melon with the tip of a knife, scoring lightly. Cut according to the diagram, poking deep into the melon (fig. 3).

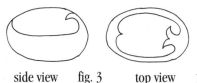

side view   fig. 3   top view

Pull the halves apart. Scoop out the flesh and save it. Make sails for the boat by poking fondue skewers through paper cut in sail shapes. Poke the skewers into the base of the watermelon (fig. 4). To make the boat fancy, line the gunwales with strawberries or grapes attached with toothpicks. Cut round holes in the sides for portholes.

Then fill the boat with assorted fruit like cantaloupe and honeydew cubes, grapes, strawberries, and raspberries. Don't forget to add the watermelon you saved earlier. And make sure your portholes are smaller than the fruit pieces, or you'll lose your cargo in the sea! Place the ship on a bed of flaked coconut tinted blue.

fig. 4

King Triton's Concert

When the mermaids and mermen arrive, the first order of business is to prepare for King Triton's concert. To do this, the guests must make instruments.

For the percussion section, use pairs of paper bowls stapled together with noisemakers inside. The fun part is decorating the bowls with crayons, markers, adhesive stickers, and ribbons. Let the guests pick out what kinds of noisemakers they want inside their bowls. Plastic buttons sound different from pebbles, styrofoam pieces will make a light, swishing noise, while one large, crumpled ball of foil will give a clean, clear percussion beat. Experiment with noisemakers around your house to find the most interesting assortment of sounds.

It's a good thing this party isn't *really* under the sea, or these instruments would be mush!

A concert has to have more than percussion, so here's how to make wind instruments. Save empty juice and soda bottles and fill them with lemonade to different levels. Show the mermaids and mermen how to blow across the tops for different musical tones. Make sure each child has a percussion instrument and a wind instrument before the concert begins.

If you can get the soundtrack for *The Little Mermaid*, play portions of it and let the mermaids and mermen accompany it with their instruments. Without the soundtrack, you will have to direct the music.

Let the children shake their paper bowl noisemakers to the beat, but tell them they can only blow on their bottles when you point to them. See what kinds of songs you can create!

When the concert is over, all the musicians get awards for an excellent performance, and get to drink the lemonade in their bottles.

What Is It?

After the concert, it's time to check out Ariel's collection of human things. But Ariel's problem is that she doesn't know the names of the human things she has collected. And neither do your guest mermaids and mermen.

To help Ariel learn about human things, use pictures of common household items cut from magazine and newspaper advertisements. Cut out one picture for each guest, and paste each picture on an index card. If you can find enough different pictures, make two cards for each person.

Put all the cards in a fish bowl and let each person choose one. They must find the object in the room that matches the picture on their card. Picture matching is the easiest way for young children to figure out "What is it?"

Before the party, tape small wrapped prizes to the objects that correspond to the pictures. When the guest matches his picture of, say, a telephone, to the real phone in the room, he'll immediately be rewarded with a prize.

For younger children, wait until the first child has found his object before the second child picks from the fishbowl. This eliminates confusion and lets the waiting children "help" the looker by offering suggestions like, "Go by the door," or "Maybe on the couch." The only rule is that the helpers can't mention the object by name.

Hidden Shells

Help Ariel add to her collection by finding beautiful seashells. If you live near the shore, collect small shells that line the water. Or, buy them in bulk in discount and hobby stores. Hide them all over before your guests arrive. Let the mermaids and mermen hunt for shells until they're all found, or until a certain time limit is reached.

The one who finds the most shells gets the prize. Award a special prize for the mermaid or merman who finds the only cat's eye shell—the kind of shell Ursula used to capture Ariel's voice (fig. 5).

fig. 5

After finding seashells, the mermaids and mermen can make their own seashell necklaces, like the one Ursula made out of Ariel's voice shell. Craft stores sell packs of shells that already have holes in them for threading. Use embroidery thread and dull-nosed needles to keep this activity safe.

If your mermen aren't excited about necklaces, let them create shell pictures with stiff paper and glue. With a little imagination, shell arrangements can become landscapes, flowers, and animals.

Guess My Name

Ariel's collection of human things makes her want to live with humans. She sees Eric and falls in love. But for a chance to court him, she must give up her voice. Since she can't speak, Eric has to guess her name.

Cut out three pictures each of the characters in *The Little Mermaid* from a coloring book. Use one character for each guest: Ariel, Eric, Flounder, Sebastian, Ursula, King Triton, Jetsam, Flotsam, Grimsby, Charlotta, and Ariel's six sisters, Lanaa, Ledala, Narandi, Aqaatu, Anitta, Riatas.

Hold up one picture and ask if anyone can guess the name. Whoever guesses right gets the picture. If someone guesses right twice, that child must give his second picture to someone who doesn't have one.

After everyone has a picture, they can use them to find their places at the party table. Before the party, string styrofoam balls painted bright colors onto long pieces of fishing line. Thread a darning needle with the line and you can easily poke through the balls. Space the balls to hang on the line every couple of feet. Make one line of balls for each guest, using one color of balls on each line. Twine them around the room, but don't cross them too much. Tape the second picture at the beginning of each line.

Have the guests find the picture at the end of a line that matches their picture. They follow the fishing line all around, until it ends at a chair at the party table. To make sure everyone is at the right place, place the third *Mermaid* character picture at each place setting at the table. To celebrate a successful end of the trail, nestle a small wrapped gift in a folded napkin near each place card.

Crab for Dinner

Serve fun finger foods like fried fish sticks or popcorn shrimp. Give them a taste of "seaweed" which is actually cooked spinach. Pass around bowls of tiny fish-shaped crackers, and, of course, let them dig into the cargo in Eric's watermelon boat.

Remember how Sebastian almost became a crab dinner? Astound your mermaids and mermen by serving a golden-brown crab-shaped bread. Buy raw bread stick dough or make bread dough from your favorite bread recipe.

If you start with breadsticks, get the large package of eight soft sticks. Knead four of them into a ball and flatten it into a circular mound. Knead the other four sticks into three equal-sized dough balls. Take two of the

fig. 6

balls, flatten them and cut a slit from the center to one edge. Pull open the slits. Cut the last ball of dough into eight pieces and roll each piece into a cylinder. (fig. 6) shows all the dough pieces before assembly.

Grease a baking sheet and assemble the pieces on the sheet as shown in (fig. 7). Bake at 375 degrees until golden brown. Cook spinach noodles and mound them on a large platter. Nestle the baked crab in this bed of "seaweed." Be careful not to break the crab claws during transport.

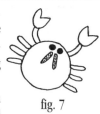

fig. 7

Use toothpicks to attach black olives for eyes. Push in two pretzel sticks for antennae. Your mermaids and mermen won't be crabby when they eat this crab!

You can even take this treat a step further, and make a small individual crab for each guest.

Seashell Cake

Then, delight your mermaids and mermen with a chocolate seashell cake. Bake a round or rectangular cake and frost it with blue icing. Sprinkle pastel candy pieces on the top for a dainty appearance.

To make chocolate shells, cover a rippled scallop shell with tin foil. Press the foil tightly, so all the bumps and ridges show clearly. Melt candy-mold chocolate in a double boiler and use a pastry brush to paint the outside of the foil-covered shell with chocolate. The chocolate will harden in a few minutes. To make it easier to handle, place it in the refrigerator until the chocolate is hard. Then pull the foil off the shell, and peel the chocolate off the foil. The chocolate will pick up every ripple from the foil mold and look like a real seashell.

Make several shells and arrange them on top of the cake. Place one shell where each cake slice will be, or make a cluster in the center. For a lighter touch, buy chocolate pieces in pastel colors and make rainbow shells.

Ursula the Octopus Cake

If your mermaids and mermen are into adventure, treat them to an Ursula the Octopus cake. Bake two round cake layers and cut one layer into octopus legs as in (fig. 8). Arrange the leg pieces around the uncut layer. Frost it all in chocolate. Add miniature marshmallows for eyes and a mouth, and use flat pink table mints for suction pads on the legs (fig. 9). After eating this cake, your guests won't be able to say they don't like octopus!

fig. 8

Mermaid Prizes

It's easy to round up theme-related prizes for Disney shows. For *The Little Mermaid*, give out sets of shell-shaped bath soaps, and sponges. That is, *real* sponges they sell in bath shops that specialize in natural items. To save money, buy one large sponge and cut it into pieces to make several prizes. Or, give imitation sponges shaped like sea creatures. Real seashells, seahorse skeletons, and dried starfish are good prizes.

For the sweet tooth, give a variety of oyster "pearls"— gum balls, sour balls, and jawbreakers. Gummi fish, sharks, and worms are always a favorite. And don't forget to give out packs of goldfish crackers.

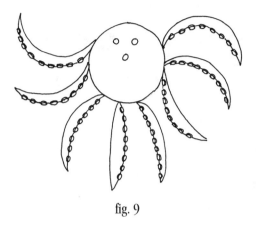

fig. 9

After a day with Disney, your mermaids and mermen and your special birthday child will be as happy as Ariel and Eric. And any Disney film your child loves will work the same magic.

PART THREE

Themes Geared for Middle Aged Kids

By the time your child is six to eight years old, planning parties has probably left you feeling middle aged. But don't let the prospect of another birthday get you down.

These themes focus on favorite topics for six- to eight-year-old children. They take your birthday child to the jungle, to the West, to the ball field, the pool, and even into outer space. These parties are sure to satisfy even the most adventurous child—without leaving the backyard!

7

Tell Me a Story

Most children have stories they want read to them over and over, and have books that are worn ragged from use. Delight your child with an entire birthday party based on a treasured story.

You can use any story your child loves, but for this example, we'll use *The Black Stallion*, a story that has been popular with children for over fifty years. Its horse theme is a winner with children of all ages.

A Shipwreck

The story of the black stallion begins with a shipwreck on a desert island, so announce the party with desert island invitations. The finished invitation looks like (fig. 1). Here's how to create it.

Start with a plain square piece of tagboard cut to fit into an envelope. Draw a large oval where the "island" is going to be. Write the party information around the oval, in the water, leaving some space on top for the tree.

fig. 1

At the grocery store, buy a roll of blue-tinted plastic wrap. Cut out a piece to cover the whole card and attach it by ironing like this: Cover your ironing board with a brown paper grocery bag cut open and laid flat. This will keep the hot plastic from sticking to your ironing board. Then lay the blue piece of plastic on the paper and the invitation face-down on the plastic. With your iron on medium-high heat, press the invitation. But only press down for an instant. If you iron too long, the blue plastic will stick to the paper bag *and* the invitation. With quick heat, the plastic will only stick to the invitation, creating ripply, blue water.

Next, cut the oval "island" out of a piece of medium-grained sandpaper, and glue this on. Finally, cut a palm tree out of construction paper and glue it on the island, being careful not to cover up the words.

But if your child's friends don't know much about the story of the Black, they might wonder what an island has to do with it. So get right to the point with horse head invitations. Use black construction paper for the horse, and light-colored paper like yellow or white for the bridle, so the writing on it will show up clearly. Glue on a paper eye and a yarn mane (fig. 2).

In your invitation, suggest that the parents of the invited children read the story of The Black Stallion to them before the party. Or the children can check the book out of the library and read it themselves. Knowing the background of whatever story you use will make your party more exciting.

fig. 2

The Stable

Invite the guests in with a huge horse head on the front door. Black tagboard and bright red ribbon for the bridle makes an eye-catching poster. Add a sign saying, "The Black Welcomes You."

Here's the kicker. If you can get or make an audio tape of a horse nickering, play it when each guest knocks on the door. Then give your side of the door a kick. They'll think the Black really *is* welcoming them!

Decorate the room to look like a stable tack room. It's easy to find pictures of horses to copy from coloring books. Bring in rope from the garage to hang on the walls. If you don't have a pitchfork, use a garden fork, and lean it in a corner with a feed pail next to it. The best thing is to move most of the furniture out of the way and replace it with straw bales. You can find straw at a garden center. Put plastic on the floor first, to make cleaning up stray straw easier.

If you know of anyone who owns a horse, see if you can borrow a few things for the afternoon, like a saddle or two, a couple of bridles, and blankets. All these things will add an authentic touch to the Black Stallion's tack room.

Black Stallion Puppets

The arrival activity for this party is Black Stallion puppets. All it takes is black socks, black felt, black yarn, buttons, and glue. Give each child a sock. Let them cut out horse ears from felt and glue them onto the sock at the heel. Cut pieces of black yarn to glue on for the forelock and mane, and use buttons for the eyes. When they are finished, each child will have his own stallion to take home.

Title Toss

Every story must begin with a title. In this game, the children must spell out the title of your theme story.

Divide them into two teams, and have each team sit in a circle on the floor. Each team gets a pair of dice. The first child tosses the dice once, then hands them to the next person in the circle. Every time the total of the two dice equals an even number, they call out "even" and get a letter of the story title.

For younger children who have a difficult time with addition, give them one die, and award a letter each time they toss an even number.

You can keep score on a large sheet of paper with a line down the middle. You will have to be alert to add letters to each team's growing title as they yell out "even!" each time they get a good roll. The team that spells *The Black Stallion* first is the winner.

You can play this game more than once, spelling out names of other characters in the story, like "Alec Ramsay," "Henry Daily," or "Cyclone and Sun Raider."

Sea Rescue

In the beginning of *The Black Stallion,* Alec and the Black are rescued from the desert island. Alec must swim under the Black with straps to lift the Black to the boat. Let the children rescue their own "pasta horses" from the "sea" with spoons.

Start with a large bowl filled with cooked spaghetti noodles. Have a little water in the bowl, so the noodles don't stick together. Give each child a spoon and have them gather around the bowl. If it's too crowded, use two bowls of noodles. With everyone fishing at once, see who can use their spoon to scoop the most noodles out of the bowl.

When all the pasta is fished out, the child with the most rescued noodles wins. Noodles don't look much like horses, but they're just as hard to rescue.

Horse and Rider

The Black stallion had to be trained before he could race. This game tests how well the "horses" at your party are trained. The game is played in pairs, outside.

One child from each pair is the horse and the other is the rider. The rider holds a piece of string or rope in each hand. The horse, standing in front with his back to the rider, holds the other ends of the strings. These horses are skittish, so you'll need to use blindfolds.

Line up the horses and riders at the starting line. On "go," the riders must race their horses across the lawn, around a distant object, like a clothesline post or shed, and back. Since the horses are blindfolded, the riders must guide them by pulling on the reins.

If you have limited space, or must race indoors, send the riders around one by one and determine the winner by timing them. Award first, second and third place.

Horse Race

Once the horses are trained, it's time for the real race. This is a board game in which luck is an important factor.

Draw the game board on a piece of tagboard as the illustration shows (fig. 3). Make as many lanes as players; the example is for six horses. Use anything you want for game pieces— buttons, raw pasta, or checkers. But it's most fun if everyone can race a little plastic horse around the track, and keep their horses when the game is over.

fig. 3

Give every race horse a name. Of course, the birthday child gets to race the Black, and others can pick horse names from the story, like Sun Raider, Cyclone, Chang, or Napoleon. Or, they can use names from other Black Stallion novels, like Flame, Black Minx, or Satan.

Here's how to run the race. Shuffle a deck of playing cards and hand a card to each player. Then, draw cards from the deck one by one to send the horses around the track. Each time the drawn card matches a player's card by number or suit, that player moves his horse ahead one space.

For example, if a four of clubs is drawn from the deck, any player with a four of diamonds, four of hearts, or four of spades moves ahead. Also, any player holding a club of any denomination also moves ahead. First horse across the finish line wins.

Taking Care of the Black

After the race, all the horses must be cooled down, groomed, watered, and fed. For this game, half the children are grooms, and half are horses.

The horses line up at one end of the room, the grooms at the other. On a table near the grooms is all the equipment to take care of the horses: cups of water, apples, combs, and cooling blankets (towels).

At the start signal, each groom grabs a cup of water and brings it to the horse—without spilling it. The horse drinks all the water, and the groom runs back to the table, replaces the cup and grabs an apple. The horse must take three bites from the apple to be properly fed after the race. The groom returns what's left of the apple, picks up a comb and combs the horse's "mane." Ten strokes will be a good grooming. Finally, after returning the comb, the groom grabs a towel and drapes it over the horse's shoulders to keep the horse warm.

The quickest groom and best-mannered horse get the prize, but make sure all the grooms and horses get some kind of reward. Switch horses and grooms and play again.

Feeding time

After the Black wins the race, he gets to eat his victory oats. But your guest horses will get more than oats. When it's time for lunch, give each child a plate filled with all the Black's favorite treats: corn, apples, oats, and a couple of sugar cubes. But you can do more than serve these things plain. Serve corn-on-the-cob, candy corn, sliced apples with caramel sauce, apple crisp, and oatmeal cookies.

And don't forget the horse chestnuts. Use real chestnuts to represent the horse chestnuts found on a horse's inner foreleg.

Make sure your horses save room for the cake. Real horses don't eat cake, but these horses will devour an island cake or a Black Stallion cake.

Island Cake

To make an island cake, start with a regular round or rectangular cake. Frost it with blue icing, swirling it to make ocean waves. Make the island out of a pile of brown sugar, rounded to a flattened dome. Poke a leafy stalk of celery into the sugar for a desert island palm. Make sure to push it down into the cake far enough so it doesn't fall over. Add a small plastic horse to the island.

Black Stallion Cake

You can transform a round chocolate cake into the Black by cutting it as the diagram shows (fig. 4).

fig. 4

Discard the half-moon sliver (or eat it), and move the two triangle pieces to the top of the head for ears. You might want to cut off the bottoms of the ears to make them smaller. With such big ears, your guests would think you made a mule, instead of a stallion!

fig 5

Finish the Black by icing it with chocolate frosting. Use a chocolate candy for the eye. Make reins out of red licorice, and the mane and forelock out of black shoelace licorice. Use a knife to mark the nostrils and mouth (fig. 5).

Race Day Prizes

When your horses, riders, and grooms are finished celebrating their victory at the racetrack, it's time to go home. Make sure your guests all have plenty of race day prizes.

Small plastic horses are valued prizes. You can also give out extra horse treats—oatmeal cookies and candy corn. If you've done a good job on your horse posters, these will make wonderful prizes, too.

As the children arrive, pay close attention to their reactions to your decorations. If they "ooh" and "ah," you will know you have valuable prizes on your walls. Cut out pictures of horses from magazines and frame them in inexpensive frames.

Award ponytail holders to the girls and combs to the boys so they can keep up with their own grooming. To symbolize the wreath of roses the Black wins, give each girl a single silk or plastic rose for a prize. Award the boys inexpensive pocket knives like the one Alec used to save his life when the Black dragged him onto the island.

From this example, you can see how an entire party can be built around a single story. Use your child's favorite story and let your imagination take over.

Jungle Fantasy

What child hasn't dreamed of leading a safari through the jungles of Africa, or of hunting big game in the Amazon tropics? If your child has had fantasies like this, bring those dreams to life with a wild jungle birthday party!

Banana Invitations

For invitations that are more fun than a jungle of monkeys, write with permanent markers on real bananas. Don't press too hard, or you'll bruise the bananas. Hand deliver these edible invitations.

If it's too inconvenient to deliver your invitations personally, make lion faces you can slip into envelopes. Draw lines around the edges for the mane, and write the information around the circle (fig. 1).

Welcome your guests with a poster of your child's favorite jungle beast on the front door. A fierce lion, striped zebra, or colorful tropical parrot can invite them in with a speech balloon. "Come on in for a rip-ROARING party!" the lion

fig. 1

says. Or, "You'll have a WILD time!" says the zebra. The parrot could tell them, "Polly wants YOU to come to this party!"

Your Jungle Home

As they step inside, your guests will feel as though they've truly entered a tropical jungle. Cover the walls with trees cut from large posterboard or craft paper. Add paper snakes dangling from the branches and crawling along the wall's baseboard. Using pictures from coloring books as a guide, cut out lion and tiger faces. Cut some of the faces in half, from forehead to chin. Tuck these half-faces behind the tree trunks so they can peer out at your guests.

Trees on the walls are a good start, but they make a forest, not a jungle. Create the jungle by adding dangling vines. Make vines quickly by taping twisted green streamers in loops from one tree branch to another. Boldly stretch loops from one wall to another. Make skinny vines with green yarn looped and intertwined with the paper vines. If you have time, make more authentic-looking vines by cutting leaves from green construction paper and stapling them to your yarn vines.

You can make jungle snakes as three-dimensional as your trees by stuffing old panty hose with newspapers or rags. Cut the legs off at the top and sew the open end closed. Glue on black felt eyes and a red or black felt tongue. Drape the snakes over the furniture and twine them around chair legs. A snake hanging from the chandelier or ceiling fan will give the guests an unexpected thrill.

Almost every fabric store carries jungle-print cloth. This means you can usually find

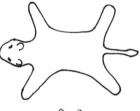

fig. 2

jungle-print remnants on the discount table for a dollar or two a yard. Use a bold leopard skin pattern or vibrant zebra stripes to cover your dinner table.

To go all out, buy a remnant of fake tiger fur. Cut the piece into the shape of a tanned tiger skin. Use scraps to add ear tufts, and sew on button eyes. Then, tack it to a wall (fig. 2). When they see this, your guests will know they've entered the domain of a great jungle hunter!

fig. 3

To add more interest to your table, draw lion faces on the paper plates with nontoxic, permanent markers, and cut manes around the edges to look like the drawn ones on your invitations. Cut squares from jungle-print cloth to use for napkins. Stuff the napkins into napkin rings made out of paper towel tubes cut into two-inch lengths. Color the tubes with markers to look like a snake skin (fig. 3). Traditional snake colors are black, brown, and gold.

Snake Socks

Many people think snakes are scary, slimy creatures. But you can prove them wrong by making cuddly, friendly snakes at your jungle party. It's another chance to get rid of those odd socks you don't know what to do with, but don't want to throw away.

These are made the same way as your larger panty hose snakes. Since odd socks by definition come in an assortment of colors and sizes, let the children begin by picking out the color snake they want to make. If there is competition for prime snake socks, choose who gets first pick by who is wearing the most jungle-theme clothes—green socks, brown pants, or a yellow and black checked shirt. Anyone who is wearing jungle-print clothing gets a special prize. You can suggest in your invitations that the guests wear jungle-theme clothes to make it a little crazier.

Provide a huge pile of rag strips to use for stuffing the snakes. White and light-colored snakes can be dressed up with patterns drawn with green, yellow, red, brown, and black markers. Let the children look at snake pictures in books to get ideas of how different snakes look.

When they see pictures of multi-colored corn snakes, the red spots of Russell's viper, and the brilliant green and white of the emerald tree boa, your guests are sure to be curious about them. Be ready to answer questions about these reptiles. Let them learn about snakes while having fun. Have a box of buttons to provide an interesting assortment of eyes for their snakes. Use pieces of string to glue on for tongues.

Snake in the Grass

After making snakes, let the children become snakes. If you're playing inside, arrange the furniture to create an obstacle course. But for this game, the snakes don't go over the obstacles, but under them. Use chairs, coffee tables, or a board laid across two pieces of furniture to create low spaces for the snakes to crawl under or through.

If you're outside, set up sawhorses, boards between ladders, or even string tied between trees or poles. Keep everything low, and close together, to keep the snakes slithering. Divide the snakes into two teams, and time each snake as they slither through the obstacle course one by one. Add the total time for each team; the team with the fastest total time wins.

Insect Buzz

Real jungle explorers often say that the worst part of the jungle is the insects. Hopefully, there won't be insects in your jungle, but it will sound like it when you play this game.

Give each child the name of an insect that makes noise, like a mosquito, fly, or hornet. As you give out names, have each child give a practice buzz. Some insects have a high whine, and others a low, bumbling buzz. Offer helpful hints, like "That sounds more like a grumpy wasp to me! Higher!" or "Is that deerfly taking a nap?" Use a light, teasing tone to get your insects giggling.

When everyone has their buzz well-practiced, the game can start. The object is to buzz the longest without laughing. Have the insects sit in a circle. At the count of three, everyone starts to buzz. The insects can make faces at each other to try to get each other to laugh, but no touching is allowed. The last one still buzzing is the winner.

If you play more than once, mix up insect names so everyone can try out different buzzes.

Scampering Chimps

Every jungle movie has lots of chimpanzees swinging in the trees and scampering along the ground. See how well your guests can run like movie chimps.

Divide the children into teams and run this game as a relay. The chimps must hold their ankles and run to a designated goal and back, without letting go of their ankles. If they let go, they have to go back to their team and start again. They tag the next chimp on their team, who grabs his ankles and scampers off. The fastest team of chimps rules the jungle!

Animal Voices

How many times has the heroine in a jungle movie been frightened by nighttime jungle noises? Wildcats roar, birds scream, elephants trumpet, and rhinos huff and snort. The heroine listens tensely, terrified by creatures she can't see.

Your guests will quickly evolve from chimps to humans to play "Animal Voices," and hear animals in the night. One person is the hero or heroine and the rest of the children are animals. The animals sit in a circle, with the heroine standing in the middle. Blindfold the heroine to create the jungle night. Turn the heroine around several times, then have her point to one of the animals in the circle and tell that animal to make an animal noise.

The commands could be, "Roar like a lion," "Talk like a parrot," or "Chatter like a monkey." The heroine must guess who is making that noise.

Let the heroine point to five different animals, giving five noise commands. She can have every animal make the same noise, or try different noises. Every time she guesses a name right, she gets a prize. Give every animal a turn at being the hero or heroine.

Feed the Parrot

After a long night in the jungle, it's time for breakfast, and the parrots are hungry. This game requires one large package of nuts and two parrots. You can make parrots out of empty jars or large disposable plastic cups.

Cut wings, tails, beaks, and eyes out of colorful felt and glue them to the jars according to the diagram. Marker lines will add details to the wings and tail (fig. 4).).

Before the party, hide brazil nuts or other large nuts all over the jungle. When it's time to feed the parrots, divide the children into two teams, and give each team a parrot. Send them searching for the nuts. The

fig. 4

members of each team put their nuts into their parrot. When all the nuts are found, the fullest parrot wins.

Monkey Meat and Tropical Eggs

After the parrots have had breakfast, it's time for the jungle explorers to eat. Start by washing the parrots' nuts and add them to a bowl of tropical fruit made of sliced bananas, melons, flaked coconut, raisins, and sunflower seeds. If you want to splurge, add special fruits like kiwis, mangos, and star fruit.

Monkey meat burgers are the main course. These are really sloppy joes, but you can add bits of red and green peppers, and chopped onions to make them more interesting. With the main course is a jungle foliage—romaine lettuce and large fresh spinach leaves. Liven it up with a dressing made of 4 tablespoons of vinegar, 2 tablespoons of sugar, and 2 tablespoons of water. Mix the vinegar, sugar, and water until the sugar is dissolved and toss with the greens.

Serve tropical eggs on the side. These could be jelly beans, malted eggs, or other egg-shaped candies.

Snake Cake

Finish the meal with a snake cake. Bake an angel food cake in a fluted pan. When the cake is cool, cut it into three layers, and cut all the layers in half, creating six half-circles. Use a serrated knife and saw gently (fig. 5).

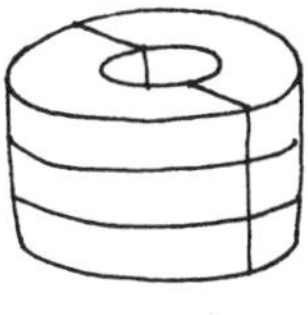

fig. 5

Arrange the half-circles end to end in alternate curves. Or, be creative and let the snake curl every direction. The sponginess of angel food lets you work with the pieces without them breaking into snake bits (fig. 6).

It's easiest to frost this cake with whipped cream tinted with green food coloring. Use purple grapes for eyes, and run a line of birthday candies down the snake's back.

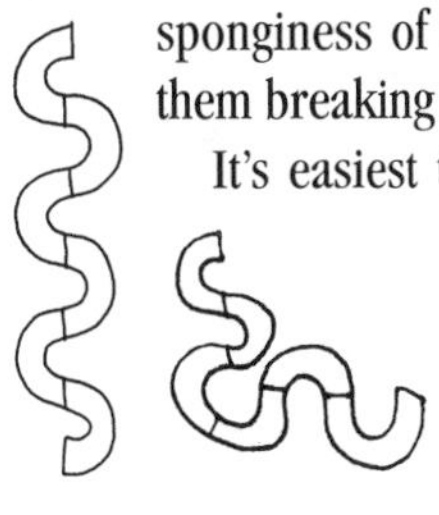

For another delicious jungle cake, instead of the snake, decorate a flat cake or a regular round layer cake with gummi worms for snakes, green coconut for grass, and arrange collard greens or kale around the base for more tropical foliage. Tuck a few jelly beans into the greens for snake eggs.

fig. 6

Jungle Trophies

Your jungle explorers will go home with wonderful trophies. Jungle prizes can included gummi worms (snakes), zoo animal crackers, and fruit-shaped candies. Give small plastic animals, and larger ones for special prizes. Small stuffed lions and monkeys are popular if your budget allows, or give tropical silk flowers.

The explorers will also be fascinated by exotic fruits like papaya, mangoes, pomegranates, tangerines, and nectarines. Their parents, too, will appreciate this healthful touch.

After surviving an afternoon of enormous insects, poisonous snakes, and fierce lions, your jungle conquerors will have earned every reward!

9

Wild West Roundup

Bring back the days of sheep herding, cattle branding, and open camp-fires with a wild west birthday. If your child likes to dress up in chaps and hat, enjoys western movies and stories, and calls you "pardner," this is the party for you.

Outlaws Wanted

Invite your child's favorite outlaw friends with wanted posters that are sure to get their attention. Write on buff-colored paper and carefully burn the edges for an old time, rustic look. The script could say, "Wanted: Dead

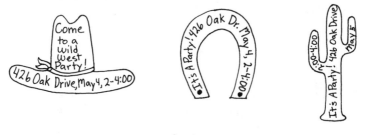

fig. 1

or Alive, Kathy Clark. Turn yourself in to Sheriff Mark at 426 Waterway Drive, 2:00 P.M.-4:00 P.M., Sat., May 28. Reward: A wild western party."

Colored paper cut into western shapes like cowboy hats, cactuses, and horseshoes also make dad-burned good invitations (fig. 1).

Indoor Desert

Your home can become any western location you choose with the proper sign on the front door. A piece of cardboard or wood that says, "The Tom L. Ranch," or "Welcome to Tumble Weed City," will give the chosen locale. Use a black marker to draw cracks and knotholes on the sign to give it a weathered wood look (fig. 2).

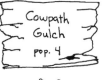

fig. 2

Inside, hang large paper cutouts of saguaro cactuses, prickly pear, mesquite, and other desert plants. Hang cardboard horseshoes painted gray over the doors for luck, and decorate other blank walls or doors with cowboy hats and boots cut from poster paper.

Check the remnant tables in your fabric store for inexpensive western-print cloth. Get a piece of red-checked fabric to use for a table cloth. Fabric with horses, cows, or cowboy designs will add to your western look when you drape them on the walls, over furniture backs, and arrange them on tables and shelves.

See if anyone you know has camping lanterns or oil lamps you can borrow. They add an authentic effect just sitting there, but it's even better if you light them during the party. However, make sure to keep them up in high places so they won't be knocked over.

Do you have any cowboy hats or boots in your closet? If you do, bring them out. Or better yet, wear them to the party. Also wear jeans, a plaid shirt, and belt. You'll fit into the scene like a fly on a cow's ear.

Around the Campfire

When cowboys worked the range, their meals were cooked over an open campfire. Give your table that authentic out-of-doors look by having a campfire in the middle of the table! Wait—calm down—the fire's not real.

Gather sticks from your yard and break them into 8-inch pieces. You might want to wash them to get rid of any clinging dirt or insects. Collect stones for the fire ring, too. Place the stones in a circle in the center of the table. Crumple up black and red paper scraps to simulate coals, and put them in the middle of the fire ring. Then, arrange the sticks on the coals to look like a campfire. Cut red and yellow flames from construction paper and poke them between the sticks. A little glue will keep the flames in place.

Checked cloth napkins are appropriate for a western table. You can make your own by cutting squares off the end of your checked tablecloth material. Fray the raw edges of the napkins for a more rustic effect.

Encourage the children to wear western clothes if they have them. As they arrive, notice their outfits and give a prize to the most authentic-looking cowpoke. To make sure everyone wins, give awards for the most colorful outfit, the coolest hat, or best boots. Be creative in thinking up award categories.

Mini-Horses

But it takes more than clothes to make a cowboy. A true cowboy must have a horse. Your guests can make stand-up horses out of clothespins, construction paper, markers, yarn, and glue.

Start with a few horse patterns made from cardboard (fig. 3). The body should be about four inches long so that the clothespin legs will be the correct proportion. Have your cowpokes trace around the patterns onto brown, white, or black paper. Next, they cut out the shapes and decorate them with magic marker eyes, nose, and mouth. Glue yarn on for the mane and tail. Two clothespins clipped to the body will make stand-up legs. Hi ho, Silver!

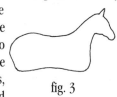

fig. 3

Cattle Rustling

One of the cowboys' most important jobs is to protect the cattle from rustlers. In this game, the cowboys get a good workout while chasing the rustlers.

To start, one player is the cowboy, one is the cattle rustler, and the rest are cows. The cows spread out and get on their hands and knees to graze. The cowboy chases the rustler as he zigzags through the cattle.

The cows try to stay away from the rustler, who tags one whenever he can. Every time he tags a cow, that cow has been "rustled" and must lie down. The object of the game is for the cowboy to catch the rustler before he has rustled all the cows.

If the cowboy catches the rustler before all the cows are lying down, he gets a reward. If the rustler rustles the herd without getting caught, *he* gets rewarded. Pick a new cowboy and rustler and play again. At the end, give rewards to all the cows, too, for being such good cattle.

Stray Cattle

In the confusion of the cattle rustling, some of the cattle broke through the fence and wandered off. Locate the lost cattle with this variation of "Pin the Tail on the Donkey."

Draw a large map with mountains, rivers, meadows, and canyons, and tack it to the wall. Add cattle to the map with adhesive cow stickers, cows cut from barnyard print wrapping paper, or hand-drawn cows. Your cows don't have to be fancy; even X's to represent cows will be fine. And you don't need many lost cows for this game. Half a dozen is plenty.

Blindfold the cowboys one at a time, and turn them around a few times. Have each cowboy try to poke a push pin into one of the lost cows. Measure the distance from each pin to the cow nearest it. The cowboy who aimed closest to a cow wins. Award a bonus for any cowboy who actually skewers a cow. Steaks, anyone?

You can add other lost animals to the map, like horses, sheep, or pigs and play again.

Branding Irons

Once the cattle are safe at home, make cattle brands that the cowboys can use to make their own printings. Help the cowboys think of good brands to use, made of combinations of letters, numbers, and symbols. Or think up brand ideas ahead of time and let your cowpokes pick the ones

Larry's Lucky Star Ranch   Mark's Circle M   Tom's Horseshoe Inn

fig. 4

they like. It's best to use at least one name initial in each brand to make them personal. (fig. 4) shows a few examples of brand designs. Have the cowboys draw their designs on cardboard, then cut them out. To make cutting easier, cut the brands out in sections that can be reassembled. For example, cut Tom's "T" separate from the horseshoe to avoid having to cut out the half-circle above the "T." Glue the cardboard brands onto smooth blocks of wood that are easy to hold. Make sure they glue the brands on *backwards* so they will print forwards.

Practice dipping the brands into shallow bowls of tempera paint and printing on paper. The cowboys can take their brands home and use them to sign letters, artwork, and make stationery, or colorful posters with multiple branding.

Cattle Branding

With the brands made, it's time to brand the cattle. One person is the cowboy, and everyone else is cattle. The cattle run around on their hands and knees, trying to avoid the cowboy. It would be easy for the cowboy to brand the cattle by tagging them, except that he's so busy pulling himself up by his bootstraps, he can't run very fast!

The cowboy must hold his bootstraps (ankles) as he pursues the cattle. He can only let go to brand a cow by tagging it. When a cow is branded, it must lay down. See how long it takes the cowboy to brand the whole herd. It's easy to time them with an egg timer, watch, or the digital timer on a microwave oven. Give everyone a turn at being the cowboy. The three fastest herd-brandings all get awards.

Chore Time

After the cows are branded, the cowboy must finish the rest of the chores. This obstacle course incorporates ranch work into a relay race.

When the relay starts, the first person on each team must put on a cowboy hat and boots, and run to his horse (a broom or mop). He straddles the horse and rides it to the watering trough (a bucket of water). At the trough, he scoops out a cup of water and sets it in front of his horse. Then he runs to the woodpile (a pile of sticks) and arranges it into a campfire. The fire built, he cooks his dinner (skewers a potato with a fork and lays the potato on the fire). Then he takes off his hat and boots and goes to bed (crawls into a sleeping bag and zips it up).

He wakes refreshed and gets up. On the way back to his team, he "undoes" everything he did so the course is ready for the next player. Carrying the hat and boots, he takes the potato off the fork, dismantles the fire, dumps the cup of water back into the bucket, and rides the horse back to the next player on his team.

The first team to finish all the chores are the stars of the ranch.

Western Cookout

After all this work, the cowboys will be hungry. Feed them a home style meal of franks and beans, and corn bread or corn muffins in a basket lined with a bandanna or red-checked napkin. Include corn on the cob and fried potatoes.

For a rib-tickling treat, cut hot dogs into bite-sized pieces, then dip them in pancake batter. Deep fry them in a fondue pot, or fill a deep skillet with enough oil to cover the pieces. Fry until golden. Your cowpokes will love these "pig bites."

Serve the food on pie pans. Serve cider in ceramic mugs. Anything with wicker, tin, or cloth will give your table the western look.

Campfire Cake

Here's how to decorate a sheet cake or round cake to look like a western prairie. First, frost the cake with green icing. Make a campfire with black jelly beans for the fire ring. Use broken pretzel sticks for the campfire, and push two or three birthday candles into the center of the fire. Push them far enough into the cake so the flames are near the "wood," but not so close that they burn the pretzels.

Stick a plastic cowboy and horse near the fire to complete the prairie-camp scene.

Sheep Cake

If you like making shaped cakes, create a sheep from a round layer cake. This is perfect for all those sheep ranchers out there.

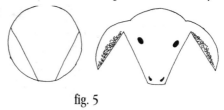

fig. 5

Cut the sides of a round cake as the illustration shows (fig. 5), and move the side pieces up and out for ears. Frost with fluffy white icing. Add raisin eyes, bits of black licorice for nostrils, and pink-colored coconut in the ears.

Cowboy Rewards

To reward your hard-working cowboys, give bandannas, beef sticks, and beef jerky for prizes. Plastic farm animals and small model horses are always popular. So are sticker books of western animals, like cows, horses, and sheep.

To make unique prizes, buy a package of chocolate pieces used for making candy molds. Melt the chocolate over low heat and scoop spoon-fuls onto waxed paper. When the chocolate cools and hardens, you'll have authentic-looking "cow pies" to give to your cow hands.

Other edible prizes are small packages of corn nuts, roasted peanuts, and barbecue potato chips.

Your cow hands will be plumb tuckered out and happy as a pig in a poke after this wild west party!

10

Play Ball!

You'll score big when you throw a birthday party filled with popular sports. Every child has a favorite sport, like baseball, football, basketball, or track and field events. Mix these together into one deluxe sports party, and everyone will be a winner.

Pennant Invitations

Give this party a hometown flavor by using your child's school colors and team as a focal point. Cut out pennant shapes from construction paper for the invitations. Use a paper punch to make a row of holes along the side and tie on yarn tassels (fig. 1).

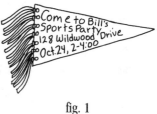

fig. 1

Team Spirit

To give your party a specific game theme, make ball invitations to match the sport you choose. Cut out white circles and use black markers to draw baseball seams. Or cut out orange circles for basketballs, or brown footballs, or white soccer balls. Let your child pick the sport and help make the invitations.

Write exciting phrases to show team spirit, like "Go, mighty Mustangs!" "Langly Lions are on the Prowl," or "North, South, East, or West, Hillview Huskies are the Best!"

If flat paper invitations aren't exciting enough for you, send invitations written on tennis balls, small foam footballs, or styrofoam balls with marker lines drawn in. On these porous surfaces, write large, using a fine-tipped felt marker to keep the lettering clear. Hand deliver them. Better yet, use real baseballs and throw them through the people's windows. Well, maybe not. That might be a little too authentic.

Banners and Pom-Poms

Keep the school theme going by decorating with balloons and streamers in your school colors. Cut pennants out of construction paper and write brief messages like, "Go, fight, win," "Touchdown!" "Two points," or "Yea, Broncos!" Banners made out of craft paper could say, "We're number one," or "Seahawks have spirit!"

It's easy to make shaggy pom-poms out of newspaper or colored tissue

paper. Lay several sheets of paper in a stack, and cut strips almost all the way across (fig. 2). Holding the uncut portion, roll the pages together into a cylinder and tape the end (fig. 3).

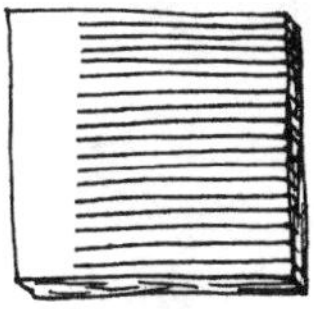

fig. 2

To make stick pom-poms, lay a dowel on the uncut end before rolling the pages, and roll the dowel into it. When you tape the handle, tape the dowel in, too. If the dowel is about a foot long, your guests will have a nice, long handle to shake.

fig. 3

Pom-poms can add a splash of color anywhere in the room—on end tables, shelves, taped in doorways or on the corners of the dining table. Tape a couple to the front door along with a banner reading, "It's Game Time at Terry's Sports Party!"

Then, decorate the room in less time than it takes to say, "Time out!" Make baseballs and basketballs by tracing around plates and bowls on colored paper. Cut them out and add the proper lines (fig. 4). Tape them on walls, doors, and mirrors.

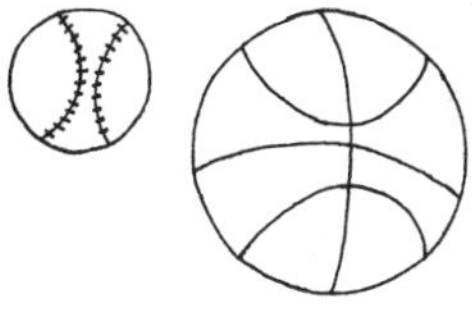

Make a centerpiece for your table with two or three pom-poms heaped in a pile. Add any small

fig. 4

sporting balls you have, or want to buy or borrow, like baseballs, tennis balls, golf balls, and ping pong balls. You can also add hockey pucks, badminton birdies, or other small sports items. Just avoid big things like basketballs that will overwhelm your table. Nestle all these things in the center of the pom-poms, and you're finished.

When your child's teammates arrive for the party, get them started making their own pom-poms. Let them all choose their favorite color paper, and have them decide whether they want to add a stick to their pom-pom. Have plenty of scissors and tape available. It's best if you have enough paper for everyone to make a pair of pom-poms. They're great to shake during the games to cheer their teammates on.

Team Tryouts

Before the games can start, the children have to try out for the team. This involves testing their skills in throwing, kicking, and fielding. Use string to mark feet and yard lines across the floor. Fasten the ends with masking tape and write the yards on squares of paper also taped to the floor.

The trick is being able to get any distance playing with balls made of crumpled pieces of paper! Give each player a sheet of tissue paper, and have them crumple them into balls. Record distances for throwing and kicking these paper balls.

Divide into pairs for fielding practice. The pairs stand facing each other at either end of the room. They each have a paper ball and throw the balls to each other at the same time. Award both teammates points when they both catch the ball. It's like basketball—you can't only score one point. Have them throw several times to accumulate points.

	throw	kick	field										total
Tom	2 yds	4 yds	0	0	1	1	0	1	0	1	1	0	11
Bill	3	2	0	0	1	1	0	1	0	1	1	0	10
Joan	4	6	1	0	1	1	0	1	1	0	0	1	16
Sally	4	4	1	0	1	1	0	1	1	0	0	1	14
Fred	3	5	0	0	1	0	1	1	1	0	0	1	13
Jill	5	1	0	0	1	0	1	1	1	0	0	1	11
Carol	5	2	0	1	0	0	0	1	1	1	0	0	11
Jack	3	4	0	1	0	0	0	1	1	1	0	0	11

fig. 5

Keep tryout scores for every team member on a chart like this (fig. 5).
When all the spaces are filled in, add the totals. Then announce the mini-
mum points needed to make the team. In this example, a player must have
at least 10 points to get on the team roster. And of course, everyone makes
the team!

Base Running

Once the team is established, the coach needs to know which players
are the fastest runners. This is important in most team sports, like baseball,
basketball, football, soccer, and hockey. Mark distances with tape or string,
or use furniture as goal markers. Have players race against each other, or
race for best time.

But these aren't ordinary running races. Have the players do forward
rolls to the goal line, then hop on the way back.

This race can also be run in a relay. Divide the players into two teams.
The first player on each team forward rolls to the goal and hops back, like
before, then tags the next person. But here's where it changes. After everyone on the team has rolled and hopped, they each take a second turn, running to the goal and crab walking back. Use your imagination to create
other modes of "running."

Balloon Basketball

Now that you know the level of each player's athletic skill, it's time for a
game of basketball. But for this kind of basketball, everyone sits on chairs!

Arrange chairs facing each other in two rows, three feet apart. Place
another chair at each end of the two rows. Make
sure there is a chair for each player (fig. 6).
Divide the players into two teams.

fig. 6

One player from each team stands on each end
chair, and holds his arms in a circle, hands
clasped, to form a basket. The rest of the players sit in the two rows of
chairs. Toss a balloon into the middle of the chairs. The players must hit
the balloon into the basket without standing up. The "baskets" can move
their arms and bodies any way they want to try to capture the balloon, but

can't step off the chair or unclasp their hands. Give two points for each basket. Play for a set amount of time, or to a predetermined point total.

After the game, make victory pennants from poster board. Let the players get ideas from your wall pennants, and add designs with markers and stickers. For flashier pennants, add glitter and sequins. Let the pennants dry while the team retires into the locker room.

Post Game Interviews

One of the most frequently asked questions when a team wins a big game is, "So how does it feel to be a champion?" This question must be asked of every player.

Tell them to think of the most wonderful, fantastic things they can imagine, or things they have always dreamed of doing, the wackier the better. Some examples might be, "It feels like riding a dinosaur through a sea of chocolate pudding," or "It feels like discovering a bottomless pit of gold in the back of my closet!"

Give prizes for the most creative answers. Let the players answer until everyone has a prize.

Off to the Airport

Next, it's time to rush to the airport to catch the plane home. Getting to the airport is never easy, especially with all the obstacles you create!

Build an obstacle course with all the challenges of a real road trip. Use masking tape to mark the course under and over furniture, and around empty boxes, with places where they must stop, or loop around. Explain that these things are viaducts, overpasses, merging traffic to maneuver around, stop signs, and cloverleafs.

Before the party, go through the course yourself, or have your child test it, and see how long it takes. Multiply this time by the number of children who will be on each team, and add a few more minutes. Say it takes two minutes to run the course, and there are four kids on each team. Give the total time for the course as ten minutes.

When the teams are ready to race for the airport, tell them they have ten minutes to get there. Each team must run the obstacle course one at a time, in less than ten minutes, or they will miss the plane.

If it turns out the players aren't as fast as you had anticipated, have the flight attendant (you) hold the plane. As the last player or two is negotiating the course, announce, "And we are experiencing mechanical trouble on runway four. Flight 239 will be delayed three minutes." This gives the teams an extra three minutes to make their flight.

They'll make it just in time!

On the plane, a meal for sports fans is served. Your hungry players have worked up a real appetite. Begin with a sports drink to replace lost electrolytes.

Basketball Salad

Then comes basketball salad. Use a melon baller to scoop out balls of orange cantaloupe. Add color to the salad with round scoops of honeydew and watermelon, along with other round fruits like blueberries and grapes. But make sure there are mostly orange balls, to keep it a basketball salad.

Yard Line Subs

For the main course, serve a long submarine sandwich filled with your favorite assortment of meats, cheese, lettuce and tomatoes. Score the top with a knife at two inch intervals. Press black shoelace licorice into these shallow cuts to mark yard lines along the length of the sandwich.

Tape or glue flag-shaped construction paper to toothpicks, and write 10, 20, 30, etc., on each flag. Push the picks in at each licorice yard line. To serve, cut in two-inch slices, using the licorice as a guide.

Sports Treats

On the side, serve round cookie cutouts decorated like baseballs and basketballs. Make baseball bats out of breadsticks by rolling one end of the dough between your palms to make it thin with a point. Push the point into a blob to make the knob of the bat (fig. 7). Bake as usual.

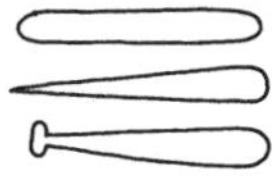

fig. 7

Football, Baseball, and Basketball Cakes

Make the birthday cake look like a playing field by icing a regular rectangle cake with green to look like grass, and draw yard lines with decorator tubes of white icing. Make goal posts out of straws. Cut a slit in the center of two straws, and slide a third straw into the slits to make the post cross beam. Push the two upright posts into the cake. Add plastic football players or soccer players to the field. Finish it by placing birthday candles along the yard lines.

If you frost the cake in chocolate, you can use white icing to make lines that look like a basketball court (fig. 8).
Make a basket on each end of the court
by stapling miniature paper baking cups
to straws. Push one straw in at each end
of the court. Add plastic basketball players.

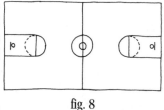

fig. 8

If baseball or softball is your child's favorite sport, start with a round layer cake and frost it in white. Add "stitches" with red or black icing on the top of the cake. You have an instant baseball! Or, you can use orange icing and black lines to make a round basketball cake.

Prizes for Everyone

In amateur sporting events, the only prize is the victory itself. But all your players are professionals. They won't get multi-thousand-dollar bonuses for each win, but they'll love these sports prizes.

For small awards, give out foil-wrapped chocolate footballs, and any round, ball-shaped candy. Give packs of gum with baseball and football cards. Larger prizes can include foam footballs, miniature basketballs, and plastic baseball bats. Even children who aren't athletes will enjoy inexpensive baseball caps, brightly patterned sport socks, and sweatbands or wrist bands.

An all-sports party gives everyone a chance to be a winner. They'll all go home feeling like champions!

11

Make a Splash

What could be better on a hot summer day than a pool party? A poolside birthday party! If you live in an apartment complex or town house with a pool, or have a private pool, you're all set. If not, check the restrictions at public pools, or head for the nearest lake. Any large body of water provides a wonderful opportunity for fun in the sun.

Sharks and Suns

The easiest invitations for a sunny party are bright suns cut from neon-yellow tagboard. Draw a smiling sun face with a black marker and write information around the circle, or in the sun rays (fig. 1).

fig. 1

If your child's pool guests are the thrill-seeking type, go with a scary shark-jaw invitation. Cut a football shape out of gray construction paper and fold the bottom third (fig. 2). Trace a line around the folded jaw and open it again. Use the line as a guide for adding white paper teeth and a red paper tongue. Draw black eyes with a marker. Write party information in the shark's mouth. Close the mouth and deliver.

fig. 2

Deep Sea Decorations

Decorate your pool scene with large gray paper sharks and colorful fish taped to the pool enclosure. Add other sea creatures like starfish, wavy weeds, and dolphins. The sample illustrations will get you started (fig. 3).

Tie green and white balloons to the pool furniture and fence. A gentle breeze will make them bob like sea bubbles. Green streamers add to the deep sea effect.

fig. 3

If your party is at the lake, tie balloons to nearby trees, and use a beach blanket for a table. On a beach that's all sand and water, mount your decorations on posts pushed into the sand.

Tropical Flowers

Next, add tropical flowers made from tissue paper. Fold several layers of paper like an accordion. One-inch folds back and forth work well. Twist a long piece of florists wire to the center of the accordion like a fan (fig. 4). Pull the paper layers apart to fluff the flower. Twist the stems to fence rails and furniture. Twist a bunch of stems together to make a bouquet for your birthday table.

fig. 4

Seaweed and Octopi

The bouquet centerpiece gives a light, cheerful feeling, and goes well with the sunshine invitations. But if you choose shark invitations, a more sinister centerpiece is in order. A big, black octopus will set the tone.

All it takes to make an octopus is a large styrofoam ball up to four inches in diameter, black yarn, some string, two buttons, and glue.

Cut the yarn into 36 pieces, each two feet long. The yarn can be shorter if you use a smaller ball. Lay the yarn in twelve piles of three. Take each bunch of three and lay them crisscross over the ball. Tie the yarn together at the bottom of the ball (fig. 5).

Braid nine yarn pieces into a three part common braid, with three strands in each part. Tie the end of this braid with string to make the first octopus leg. Braid the rest of the legs, using nine strands of yarn for each leg. Glue on button eyes.

Jumble up green streamers to make a

fig. 5

seaweed nest on the table. Place the octopus in the center of the table, its legs spread in every direction.

As your guests arrive, offer sunscreen to those who want it. Then get them started making tissue flowers like the ones you used to decorate. When the flowers are finished, set them away from the water so they won't get wet during the party.

Sink the Buoy

After making flowers, your guests will be ready to jump in the pool. But before adding this game to your party plans, make *sure* you know your guests' swimming ability. And don't wait to ask them at the party. Ask their parents when the children are invited. This way there will be no unpleasant surprises.

Before the party, blow up lots of balloons, equal numbers of blue and green ones. Divide the guests into two teams. Give them fun team names, like the Blue Barnacles, and the Green Gourami (kissing fish). Each team must sink their buoys—all the green ones or all the blue ones.

At your signal, everyone jumps into the pool and pops balloons as fast as they can. The team that pops all their balloons first, wins. Afterwards, make sure to fish out stray bits of broken balloons.

It's best to limit "Sink the Buoy" to pools, and not play it at a lake where balloons may drift out to sea, and balloon bits can be harmful to aquatic life.

Sunken Treasure

Once there are no warning buoys for incoming ships, there are bound to be sea disasters. Ships crash on the rocks and sink. It's up to your guests to retrieve the treasure these sunken ships carry.

Toss pennies into the pool and let the children dive for the sunken treasure. Each retrieved penny is worth a small prize. And they can keep the pennies, too. For less experienced divers, toss lots of coins into the shallow end of the pool.

In a lake, coins will get lost in the sand. Instead, use big rocks spray painted different colors. Your birthday child can test out rock sizes before the party, to see what size is big enough to find, without being too big to easily handle.

Be creative with rock colors. They can be gold and silver to look like money, or a rainbow of colors, like neon yellow and hot pink. Prizes can correspond to rock sizes, colors, or both.

Sun Pictures

After all that diving, it's time to dry off and warm up in the sun. Take advantage of the natural sunlight by making sun prints.

Buy a package of photo-sensitive paper from a hobby store. Give each child a piece and have them lay leaves, feathers, sticks, and rocks on the paper in interesting designs. Follow the directions that come with the paper for exposure time and washing instructions. The finished pictures will have white silhouettes on a black background.

Gone Fishing

By now your guests are probably getting hungry, but they have to catch their dinner before they can eat! Send them fishing for sponge fishes.

To prepare for this game, cut fish shapes out of colored kitchen sponges, and hook a jumbo paper clip to each fish's mouth. Each fisherman gets a long stick with a string tied on the end and another paper clip tied to the end of the string. Bend the paper clip open so it will hook the fishs' clips (fig. 6).

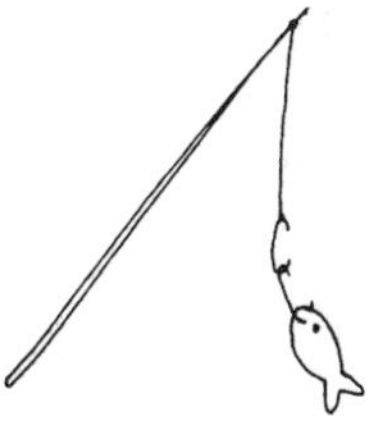

fig. 6

Toss the fish into the water, and tell your guests to go fish. At a pool, the fishermen must stay on the edge of the pool, and at a lake they must stay on shore. Keep a good eye on those sponges, so none of your fish accidentally swim out to sea!

Give prizes for each fish caught, or have the kids compete in teams like the Champion Anglers, or the Deep Sea Daredevils.

Feeding Fish

Your fishermen caught all the surface fish, but not all the ones that live way down on the bottom of the ocean. These fish live in darkness, and some don't even have eyes. It's time for your fishermen to become fish, and see what it's like to be a blind fish, searching for food without being able to see.

Toss an assortment of floating objects into the water. Anything that has no dangerous points is fine, like inflatable toys, rubber thongs, or empty plastic bottles.

Blindfold the children and guide them into the water. Set a time limit and see how many objects they can retrieve. You can let them keep the items they find for prizes, or let them trade in captured items for other things you have purchased.

"Feeding Fish" is another one of those games that should be limited to a pool party. At a lake, your blindfolded guests could wander out to sea.

Part of the fun of a pool party is just playing in the water, without planned games. Give your deep sea divers/fishermen/fish some time to have fun on their own while you get the food ready. Just make sure your guests are being supervised by a lifeguard or other adult *at all times*.

Fruit Fiesta

Make fruit kabobs with pieces of honeydew, watermelon, strawberries, grapes, and other summer fruits. Poke the pieces onto swizzle sticks or fondue sticks. For a frozen treat, poke grapes onto sticks the day before and freeze them. Keep them frozen until you're ready to serve them. This makes a tantalizing, cool treat on a hot day.

Banana Boats

Make banana boats with bananas, chocolate chips, and peanut butter chips. With the peel still on the banana, cut it open all the way down its length. Fill the slit with chips. Wrap the banana in tinfoil and let it sit in the sun during the party. By the time you are ready to eat, the chips will have melted to create a wonderful chocolate-peanut butter-banana sensation. Open the foil and peel back the peel. Make sure you bring forks. These bananas are messy!

If you have a grill or fire pit available, add marshmallows to the boat's cargo and set the foil-wrapped banana in hot coals. The marshmallows will melt for an extra-gooey s'more treat.

Danger—Sharks!

For a birthday cake that's easy to travel with, make a "Danger—Sharks" cake from a regular cake, either round or square. Frost the cake with blue icing on the top and sides. Use a knife to lift up "waves" of icing. Press fish-shaped crackers into the water on the sides.

Cut shark fins out of gray paper and poke them into the top of the cake. Then push a plastic toy man into the cake so it looks like he's drowning. Make dangerous reef rocks out of pitted prunes. Spread the blue frosting so it "splashes" onto the rocks. A sprinkling of powdered sugar makes sea foam.

Fish Cake

For a cake that doesn't promote seashore violence, make a harmless fish cake from a 9 x 12 rectangular cake. Cut the sides and tail of the cake according to the diagram (fig. 7). Turn the two side pieces around to make fins, and move the tail piece to the other end to make the head. Frost

fig. 7 it with green icing and add a chocolate candy for the eye (fig. 8). If you want, add details with shoelace licorice.

If it's a hot day, make sure there's plenty to drink. Fruit punch or lemonade with lots of ice are sure to make everyone happy.

fig. 8

Seashore Treasures

By the time the party is over, there will be water everywhere, with wet children, wet toys, and wet towels. Keep this in mind when you choose your pool party prizes.

If you want to give out packages of stickers, make sure the children don't remove the cellophane wrapper until they get home. Wet stickers are wrinkled, crumpled, ruined stickers. It's best to avoid all paper prizes, like coloring books or note pads. Stay with plastic items like small water pistols, plastic leis, or toy sharks.

And make sure to put the sun prints away with the tissue flowers for safekeeping until everyone is ready to go home. If possible, send these fragile items home in the parents' care.

Candy prizes should be wrapped in sealed, plastic packages. It's almost impossible to remove the paper wrapper from a piece of candy that's gotten wet. Good choices for pool party candy are gummi sharks and worms, and "beach ball" gum balls. Other food prizes can include picnic-type food like small packages of chips and nuts.

For larger prizes, get a few inexpensive inflatable water toys, miniature toy boats, and sun visors. Your guests will have fun with striped beach balls and other plastic balls. Almost anything that floats can be a prize.

After an afternoon of wet fun, the children will head home with seashore treasures and fun memories of a splashing-wet time!

12

The Final Frontier

Imagine a birthday filled with astronauts, space aliens, UFOs, and unexplored galaxies. This space voyage birthday will give your child an encounter of the unforgettable kind.

Space Shuttle Blast-Off

Blast off with space shuttle invitations. Roll a piece of paper into a cone and tape it onto an empty toilet paper roll. Cut slits in the sides of the "rocket" and add construction paper wings. Then, tape red and yellow curly ribbons to the end of the cardboard roll for exhaust flares. Your message goes on the rocket's body, and you can add cockpit windows, and other shuttle details with colored markers (fig. 1).

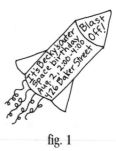

fig. 1

For a variety of invitations, cut out assorted spaceship and rocket shapes (fig. 2). Make porthole windows by gluing on circles cut with a paper punch.

fig. 2

Stars and Spaceships

A poster on your front door saying, "Welcome to the Final Frontier," will set your theme from the starting liftoff. Use black paper and write the words with white poster paint. Then add shiny star stickers, moons, and white paper-punch circles for distant stars. The final touch is to cut out a ship that looks like the Starship Enterprise and have it zooming across one corner of the poster. Not sure what the Enterprise looks like? Copy it from this handy illustration (fig. 3). Your kids will recognize it.

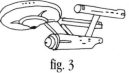

fig. 3

Indoor Universe

As your guests enter your house, spectacular outer space decorations will make them feel as though they've stepped into another galaxy. Use blue, silver, and black for your color scheme, and be generous with blue and silver balloons. Cut stars out of white paper and tinfoil to tape on walls and windows. The easiest way to make a star is to trace around a star-shaped cookie cutter. Cut out moons and planets from construction paper. Make asteroids out of crumpled up pieces of tinfoil and hang them from the ceiling with fishing line.

If your budget allows, buy small plastic models of ships, like the space shuttle and Star Trek's Enterprise, and hang them among the asteroids.

Styrofoam balls in an assortment of sizes make good planets. If you're really creative, look up pictures of the solar system in the encyclopedia, and paint your styrofoam balls to look like Mercury, Venus, Mars, Saturn, Jupiter, Uranus, Neptune, and Pluto. If you can't invest that much time, make planets quickly by wrapping the balls in foil.

On your table, use construction paper stars for place mats and cover the plates with tinfoil. Sprinkle shiny star confetti on the table.

Joining Starfleet

The voyage into space can't begin until all your arriving guests have joined Starfleet. To be an official member, each must wear the Starfleet emblem. The children can make their own official emblems to wear and become bona fide space explorers.

Before the party, make cardboard patterns of the three parts of the Starfleet emblem (fig. 4). Have an assortment of colored paper available so your explorers can cut emblem pieces out of any colors they want. It would be good to have several sets of patterns, so more than one person can trace at a time.

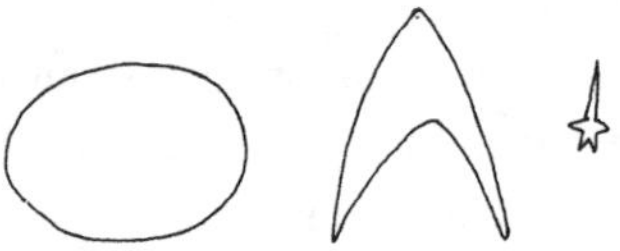

fig. 4

When each explorer has the three patterns drawn, have them cut them out and glue them together as shown (fig. 5). Fabric stores and hobby stores sell pin backs, which are like safety pins, except flat on one side. Your explorers can glue the flat sides to the backs of their emblems, let them dry, and pin them to their chests.

fig. 5

Space Voyage

Now the Starfleet crew is ready for its first voyage. Have sheets of typing paper available for the crew to fold paper airplanes. Each explorer makes his own spacecraft and can decorate it with colored markers.

Lay a huge piece of poster board on the floor. On it, draw circles labeled with planet names. Under each name put a number showing how many points that planet is worth. See whose spaceship can fly to the highest scoring planet. Toss the ships several times and award highest total scores.

Seeing Stars

During the voyage, your explorers will see lots of stars and constellations. This game tests your explorers' creativity in seeing animals and people in the patterns of stars, just like ancient people did. To prepare, get several large pieces of posterboard and draw marker dots to form outlines of objects. Draw one constellation on each poster. The illustrations will give you a few ideas (fig. 6).

Then cut out the dots, cutting a dime-sized hole where every star is marked.

When the explorers are ready to see stars, turn off the lights and shine a flashlight through the holes in the papers. Have the flashlight set up on a high shelf at one end of the room, and hold the paper a few feet from the

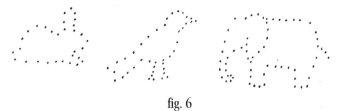

fig. 6

opposite wall. If you hold the paper at about shoulder height, the children can sit on the floor in front of your feet, and have a clear view of the stars that shine through the paper onto the wall in front of you.

The farther back the flashlight is, the more clearly the stars will show up. Before the party, experiment with distances until you find what works best.

When your explorers are all sitting on the floor, show the constellations one by one. The children call out the pictures they see. "That's a bear!" or "It's a rabbit!" To encourage even the shy children, give everyone a small prize as soon as someone makes a correct sighting.

Those Noisy Aliens

During this space voyage, your explorers will see more than stars. They'll also encounter UFOs and space aliens. These spaceships and space creatures make strange noises!

Have all the explorers sit in a circle. The first person in the circle makes a space sound, like "Beep-beep." The person next to him repeats that sound and adds another one: "Beep-beep, wheeeooo." The next person repeats those two sounds and adds a third: "Beep-beep, wheeeooo, sproink."

Each person keeps adding a sound, until someone makes a mistake. The explorer who misses a sound must go on shore leave, and leave the circle. The rest continue, until only one explorer is left to win the prize.

On this voyage, your explorers not only *hear* aliens, but see them, too. Give your explorers a chance to recreate these alien beings.

They can make all kinds of weird space creatures by sticking marshmallows together with toothpicks. Use big marshmallows and miniature ones. Dye bowls of water with food color. When the explorers dip the marshmallows in it, they will have multi-colored aliens. Set out a small bowl of raisins for eyes, black and green olives, cherries, or any soft foods that can be connected with toothpicks. You will be amazed by the strange creatures that inhabit the universe!

Asteroid Mining

Now the explorers must complete their space mission—collecting mineral samples from the asteroid field.

Divide the explorers into two teams. Each team must load their spaceship with asteroid samples. The asteroids (crumpled balls of tinfoil) are in two piles at one end of the room. The spaceship cargo bay (a pail covered in foil) is at the other end of the room. Each team forms a line between their asteroids and the cargo bay.

The explorer next to the asteroids grabs one and hands it down the line, all the way to the bay. He watches his teammates, and as soon as that asteroid is dropped in the cargo hold, he grabs another asteroid and starts it down the line.

Easy, right? But not while wearing spacesuit gloves! To protect from radiation and other harmful properties, each explorer must wear gloves. These can be oven mitts, large leather work gloves, or mittens. The bigger and clumsier the gloves, the better. If you can't round up that many pairs of gloves, plastic sandwich bags with rubber bands at the wrists will stop harmful asteroid radiation just as effectively.

Asteroid Analysis

Once the asteroid samples have been collected, it's time to take them to the space lab for analysis. Dump all the asteroids from the cargo holds into one huge container. Let each explorer pick out one asteroid. Go around again, and have them each pick a second, and third, until all the asteroids are gone.

Tell the explorers to uncrumple the foil to see what prize is hidden inside. But they must be careful not to tear the foil. You'll find out why in a minute. The asteroids that are made of valuable minerals have bigger prizes inside. Others are worthless space rocks and have no prize.

When all the asteroids have been reduced to flat pieces of foil, check the foil and give a special prize to anyone who analyzed an asteroid without tearing it.

With the asteroid mission completed, it's time for an outer space meal.

Orbit Fruit

Make orbit fruit with half an orange placed flat side down. Skewer grapes and cherries with toothpicks and poke them into the orange. For variety, add other foods like olives, melon chunks, or cheese cubes (fig. 7).

fig. 7

Give one asteroid to each guest by wrapping a handful of popcorn in a piece of plastic wrap. If you get good, sticky wrap, you won't need to use anything extra to keep it closed. For more authentic asteroids, use blue-tinted plastic if your grocery store carries it. Tape it closed on the bottom if you need to.

The Rings of Saturn

Treat your explorers to a taste of Saturn's rings. Take a slice of bread and use two different sized drinking glasses to cut concentric circles. Discard the outside scrap, but save the bread ring and the smaller inner circle, which is actually Saturn. Brush the pieces with butter, sprinkle with parmesan cheese, and bake them in the oven at 350 degrees. Give each explorer one of Saturn's rings and one planet.

Cucumber Crafts

Every explorer gets his own private shuttle when you make cucumber crafts. First, slice off one side of the cucumber so it will lie on the plate without rolling away. Trim one end to a point and cut off the other end so it's flat. Cut slits on opposite sides, close to the flat tail end. Cut a third slit in the round top. Use the scrap from the bottom to cut triangle wings. Push the wings into the three slits near the tail. Then add windows made of black olive slices, attached with toothpicks (fig. 8).

fig. 8

If the moon is made of green cheese, shuttles can certainly be made of cucumbers.

Outer Space Cake

An ordinary cake with chocolate frosting can become outer space-like if you sprinkle silver candy balls on top. Make small star-shaped sugar cookies and press them into the chocolate frosting. Add a small plastic spaceship or two.

UFO Cake

Make a three-dimensional UFO cake by baking half the cake batter in a regular eight-inch round pan and baking the rest in an oven-safe bowl with a diameter of about four to six inches. After the cake is baked and cool, invert the bowl cake on top of the round layer. Frost it with white icing. Add portals made of chocolate candy pieces and a red cherry beacon on top (fig. 9).

fig. 9

Astronaut Food and Orbit Gum

Reward these courageous space explorers with samples of "real" astronaut food. Novelty stores and camping stores sell packages of freeze-dried space food, everything from ice cream to french fries. Other space food prizes can include orbit gum, moons and planets disguised as jawbreakers and gum balls, and donut hole asteroids.

Give out frisbee flying saucers, small model spaceships, and shuttles. And don't forget space exploration equipment. Water pistols make fine laser guns. Wrap-around sunglasses become space visors, and chocolate bars wrapped in tin foil with black paper control buttons are can be communicators just like the ones the Enterprise crew uses to say, "Beam me up, Scotty!"

This outer space adventure is for anyone who is fascinated by the mysteries of the vast universe and wants to venture into the Final Frontier.

PART FOUR

Themes for Older Children, Still Young Enough for a Party

Children who are nine, ten, and eleven years old are well beyond the age when games like "Go Fish" and "Duck, Duck, Gray Duck" sound like fun. They want a more grown-up party. So here are themes which incorporate mystery, travel, nature, and religion into parties even the most mature eleven-year-old will enjoy.

Make the most of these themes before your child says, "I'm too old for a party." Your child is growing fast, but isn't grown up yet!

It's a Mystery to Me

Mysteries hold a fascination that's impossible to resist. From Sherlock Holmes to Nancy Drew and the Hardy Boys, sleuths intrigue kids of all ages. So hold a mystery birthday party that's sure to delight and thrill your own amateur sleuths.

Decoding Messages

Every part of this party has an unknown factor—a mystery to be solved—starting with the invitations. There are a number of ways to create invitations that need to be decoded to be read. One idea is to write each word backwards, or to write in numbers, with each number representing one letter of the alphabet.

You can use other forms of writing, too, like braille or Morse code. Or be really creative and make up your own language. Use geometric shapes and designs to represent letters. Or cut out pictures from magazines to represent words.

With all these code-type messages, don't forget to send decoding instructions. You'd hate to have your guests miss the party because they couldn't figure out the invitation!

But you don't have to send the decoding instructions with the invitation. Wait a day or two to let them try to decode it on their own. Then send the solution separately. It's a good idea to write a tantalizing clue on the coded invitation, so they know there is more on the way. Just a simple message like, "The puzzle will be solved in two days," or "Soon the mystery will end—and another will begin," will keep people from throwing the invitation away before the solution arrives.

Another way to make a mystery invitation is to model it after a ransom note. Piece together letters cut from magazines and newspapers. It could say something like, "Challenge your sleuthing skills at a mystery birthday party filled with curious clues and surprising solutions." Then give the day, place, and time, and draw little question marks all around.

A Mysterious Mood

Decorate the invitations with black question marks, and hang a corresponding question mark on your front door, cut out of black poster paper. Use black and white balloons and black streamers. Cut out more question marks to hang on the walls and doors.

Black place mats and black paper plates and cups will add a mysterious, sinister tone. But don't overdo it with the black, or your party will look like a funeral. Add red and white accents for a classic look.

Unknown Designs

The first mystery of the party comes from fold-and-dip place mats. Give each guest a white paper towel. Use the sturdy kind they say you can scrub carpets with, so they won't rip when they get wet. Have them fold the paper like an accordion, then fold it in half (fig. 1). Put out several bowls of water, dyed with an assortment of food coloring. The guests then dip the corners of the folded paper into the bowls of colors. Let them dip more than one paper, experimenting with different kinds of folds and different colors.

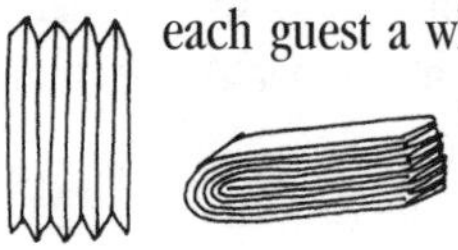

fig. 1

It's best to use clothespins to hold the paper, to keep fingers from getting stained.

When all the corners have been dipped, carefully open the paper and the hidden design will appear. Let the paper towels dry, so that each child will have a personalized place mat for the table. You might want to laminate them with a little clear contact paper to protect them. Make sure your black place mats are a couple of inches bigger than the paper towels.

Those black mats will create a dramatic frame when the fold-and-dip designs are placed on top of them.

Clue Observation

To solve any mystery, detectives must be able to find clues. Test your sleuths' powers of observation with this observation game.

First, give the sleuths one minute to look around the room, noticing as many details as they can. Then tell them to close their eyes. Blindfold them if you don't trust them to keep their eyes closed. While no one can see, move one object. When they open their eyes, see who is first to figure out what is different.

Play several times, beginning with the obvious things. Remove a picture from the wall, or take away large throw pillows. Then make smaller changes, like moving a figurine, or turning a book around.

To help confuse things, take your time making each change. While everyone's eyes are closed, walk around the room, pretending to move things. Make shuffling, tapping, and sliding sounds as you pretend to move things. Your detectives will have to listen carefully as well as observe to spot the clues!

Drawing in the Dark

Anything that happens in the dark is mysterious. When your sleuths try to draw pictures in the dark, they'll end up with finished artwork they never expected.

Give everyone paper and pencils. Turn off the lights and name an object related to mysteries. Some examples are a paintbrush (to dust for finger-prints) or a gun or a knife (murder weapon). Give them thirty seconds to draw in the dark. Then turn on the lights. The biggest detective challenge will be to try to figure out how those ordinary objects became so strange-looking!

Have them draw several objects on one sheet of paper. If the pictures overlap, it gets even more interesting.

Afterward, hang all the pictures up so everyone can see them. Award prizes for the most accurate drawing, the most mysterious drawing, and the most creative drawing. Invent any prize categories that fit the results of drawing in the dark.

Mystery Pictures

Good sleuths have to be able to take clues that don't mean anything by themselves, and put them together to create a complete picture of a crime.

Here's your sleuths' opportunity to make pictures out of mysterious clues and shapes. Before starting, cover your work table with a drop cloth or newspapers. Give everyone blank paper, paint, and paintbrushes. Each detective sprinkles paint on his paper in blobs and patterns. When the paper is folded in half, pressed flat and opened again, the paint will be spread into abstract designs.

Your sleuths' challenge will be to make sense out of these meaningless designs. Give them black markers to add details to the pictures to create animals, landscapes, and people.

Murder Mystery

Now that you know how well your sleuths can discover and work with clues, it's time to solve a murder.

Give everyone a small folded piece of paper. All the papers are blank except two: one has an "x" on it, and one has an "o." All the players open their papers, without revealing what, if anything, is written on them.

The person who has the "o" is the detective. He shows his "o" and leaves the room. While the detective is gone, the person who got "x" commits the murder. He walks to someone and touches her. That person—let's call her Sally—is killed, and lies on the floor.

The detective returns and must solve the murder. He does this by asking each person, "Did you kill Sally?" Of course, everyone answers, "No, I didn't kill Sally." Even the murderer responds this way. The detective must study each suspect carefully for nervousness, or any other signs of guilt. After he has questioned each suspect, he must guess who the murderer is.

He might say, "I think Joe killed Sally." Joe must then tell the truth. If he is the murderer, he must confess. If Joe didn't kill Sally, the detective can guess again. He can guess as often as he needs to, but the reward for solving the crime gets smaller with each wrong guess.

For example, the prize for guessing right the first time could be a pack of five rolls of candy. With the first wrong guess, the prize becomes three rolls, then two, then one. Then break the roll open and give one tiny single candy. (And give each victim and all those wrongly accused prizes, too, as compensation for pain and suffering).

Mystery Ride

Finally, take your sleuths on a trip that tests all their detective skills. Blindfold them and load everyone into the car. For a larger party, you might have to use a van. Then, drive to a distant destination. It could be a park, a shopping center, a restaurant, or the bus station. Your assistant can sit in the back to make sure no one takes off their blindfolds.

See how long it takes for them to guess where you are going. Those familiar with the neighborhood might be able to follow the turns and stops to guess. Others will have to use clues like traffic noise, smells, and other sounds. If it's too cold or rainy to drive with the windows down, have your sleuths try to guess where they are after they arrive and get out of the car. Drive to several locations, so more sleuths can win prizes.

Your party meal can begin when you return home, or pack the food in the trunk and eat at your final destination, like a park or the lake.

Puzzling Food

The mainstay of a mystery party is filled things. Foods with hidden fillings are a mystery until they are bitten into. Some examples are tortillas with different meat and cheese fillings, crepes, and filled pasta.

Brave sleuths can choose their food and be surprised with the first bite. For those who are more cautious, have them guess at the contents of each food, and reveal the mystery before they eat.

Make a mystery punch by starting with your favorite fruit flavored drink. Add ice cubes made of a contrasting drink. For example, serve cranberry juice cocktail with ice cubes made of pineapple juice. Or float lemonade ice cubes in orange juice.

Mystery Prize Cake

Your cake can carry the mystery theme, too. Add mystery surprises to each piece of cake. No one will know what they have until they dig into it.

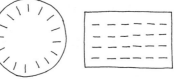

fig. 2

Bake a flat cake, either round or rectangular. When it's cool and turned out onto a serving platter, use a sharp knife to cut small slits in the top, an inch wide and an inch deep (fig. 2). Arrange the slits so that one cut will be in each piece when the cake is served.

Then cut a note card into one-inch squares. Write a number on each square. Insert the squares into the slits in the cake, and frost as usual. Score the cake where it will be cut and make a frosting question mark on each piece with decorator icing tubes (fig. 3).

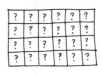

fig.3

The numbers on the papers will correspond to numbered prizes. Have the prizes displayed with their numbers, so the sleuths can anticipate cutting into the mystery cake. If you have more cake than guests, see who gets the leftovers with a drawing.

Say there are eight guests and three pieces of cake left over. Take eight slips of paper and draw a black dot on three of them. Put all the papers into a hat. Whoever draws out the papers with dots gets the extra pieces of cake. However you handle it, though, it's better to have too much cake than not enough.

Question Cake

For a cake that highlights your question mark decorations, start with a rectangle cake and cut it according to the diagram (fig. 4). Use the small square for the dot below the question mark. Frost it any way you

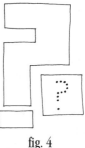

fig. 4

want, and add candles to the large extra square in the shape of another question mark.

Detective Prizes

Reward your persistent, talented sleuths with detective equipment like magnifying glasses, tweezers, note pads, and pens. Give out detective disguises, including false mustaches, plastic sunglasses, and odd hats. Nancy Drew books are popular prizes, as well as Hardy Boys mysteries and detective comics.

Candy prizes should follow the same theme as your food. Anything with filling is a mystery. Filled chocolates, hard candy with gum or soft centers, and cakes with fruit or creme fillings are all examples. To increase the mystery, wrap prizes in plain brown paper. This gives everyone the thrill of opening mysterious packages.

Like any good detectives, your sleuths won't be able to leave this party until every mystery has been solved. And they'll love solving them!

14

Here, There, and Everywhere

Buenos Dias! Hallo! Bonjour! Hop on a plane and take a fabulous trip around the world. Visit Mexico, Germany, France, China, and the Caribbean during this international birthday party.

Hop on the Plane

World travelers usually travel by plane, so send airplane invitations. You can make paper airplanes out of pieces of typing paper. First, fold the paper in half lengthwise. Holding it with the folded edge toward the bottom, fold the top right corner down toward you so the right side is even with the bottom fold (fig. 1). Fold the other top corner down the same way, but toward the back.

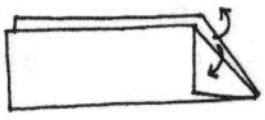

fig. 1

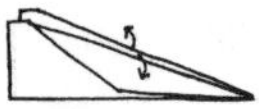

fig. 2

Then fold the *new* top right corner down again, so that the folded right edge is even with the bottom fold (fig. 2). Again, fold the other new top corner down the same way, but to the back.

Once your plane is all nicely folded, open it up again and write your message on the inside folds. Fold the plane again and slip it in an envelope. Your guests can unfold the plane to read it.

fig. 3

See the World

If you want to give your guests more party details, draw a world map on a piece of plain paper. It doesn't have to be detailed, but should be accurate enough so people will recognize the Earth, and not mistake it for a lunar landscape! Fill in the names of the countries you will be visiting, and weave the invitation message among the countries (fig. 3).

A Foreign Flair

Use a larger copy of this same drawing to hang on your front door. Color in the blue ocean and fill in continents or nations with different colors. Welcome your guest in several languages. The words "Bonjour" (French), "Buenos Dias" (Spanish), "Pronti" (Italian), and other greetings will make your travelers feel right at home.

Inside, hang road maps on the walls. If you have an old, out-of-date atlas you're willing to sacrifice, tear out the pages and hang these up, too. Local travel agents have travel posters you can have for little or nothing—as long as you don't mind the airline and hotel advertising on them.

Go to hotel and motel lobbies and pick up the travel brochures on their display racks. Better yet, tourist information places are happy to provide you with all sorts of interesting maps and flyers about things to see and do. Getting all of this information might even inspire you to go to some of these places one day.

If you get enough of these brochures, they can cover your table. Lay them edge to edge and tape them together into one huge sheet. Drape it over your dining table for an international tablecloth.

Fold paper airplanes and add colored stripes with markers to make them look like airline planes. Use fishing lines to hang them from the ceiling.

If you have any foreign clothing, trinkets, or knickknacks, now is the time to get them out. Mexican woven blankets, serapes, Chinese dolls, and painted fans will add color and style. Don't hesitate to ask friends for foreign items you can borrow.

Add more color with bright tissue paper flowers, as described in chapter eleven. Use a bundle of flowers for a table centerpiece, and arrange others so they accent foreign knickknacks.

Ojo de Dios

Your guests can get involved in an international project right away by making an ojo de dios, the eye of the gods, or god's eye. These Mexican wands are instruments of petition for the Huichole Indians of the Sierra Madre mountain range.

All it takes to make each god's eye is two dowels, one 25 inches long and the other 15 inches long, and brightly colored yarn. Start by laying the dowels side by side, so they are even at the top (fig. 4). Use a short stick, such as a wooden popsicle stick, for a smaller project.

fig. 4

Halfway down, wind yarn around both dowels and twist them so they are at right angles, making a cross (fig. 5). Then wrap the yarn around the cross the other way, to hold them in place (fig. 6). From there, keep wrapping the yarn around the sticks, over and under one stick, then over and under the next, keeping the strands close together without overlapping (fig. 7). Change yarn colors by snipping the color you're using, and tying another color to the end of the yarn. Keep wrapping colors until the short sticks are covered almost to the end. Wrap the long stick with yarn and tie it at the bottom(fig. 8).

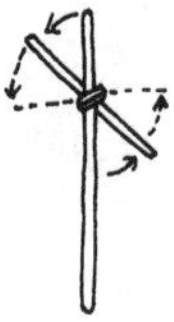

fig. 5

fig. 6

To finish the project, add tassels by laying a bunch of yarn pieces over the ends of the yarn over them to hold them in place. Tie the tassels tightly.

fig. 7

fig. 8

Foreign Travelers

Before starting on your world tour, see how much your guests know about different countries with this naming game.

Fill a paper bag, pillow case, or other large bag with an assortment of "foreign" objects. These can be almost anything. A plastic lion (Africa), a bread stick (France), a stuffed panda bear (China), a wooden-soled sandal (Holland), or a toy cow (India), are a few ideas.

Each guest picks an item out of the bag and must guess which country the item is associated with. He can have three guesses. If he still doesn't know, he can hand the object to the traveler next to him, who gets one guess. The travelers keep passing the object around until someone guesses the right country. Whoever gets the answer right gets a prize, and keeps the object to use in the next game. Play until everyone has a prize and a foreign object.

Pack Your Bags

Now that everyone is well-versed in foreign culture, it's time to pack for the trip.

Divide the travelers into two teams and have each team form a line. The first person in each line names his item and the place it comes from. For example, if he was given a lion, he says, "I'm going to Africa and I'm bringing my lion." Then he hands his lion to the person behind him. Say the next person is holding a maple leaf. He says, "I'm going to Africa and I'm bringing my lion, then I'm going to Canada and I'm bringing my leaf." Then he hands the lion and the leaf to the person behind him.

Each traveler adds to the list, and adds to the armload of stuff. This game has a double challenge—to remember everything in the list in order, and to not drop anything as the items are handed along. The last person on each team dumps his armload into a waiting suitcase. See which team can get packed the quickest.

It helps to have an assistant for this game. Since both teams are talking at once, it's best to have one person listen to one team, and the other listen to the second team, to catch packing mistakes.

Destination, Please

To see which countries your travelers will visit, play this version of "Pin the Tail of the Donkey" by pinning airplanes to a map of the world.

Draw a world map similar to the one on your front door, and tape it to the wall. Have the names of many countries marked. Also mark the locations of several airports.

Give each traveler a tack and a paper airplane cutout (fig. 9). Blindfold the travelers one at a time.

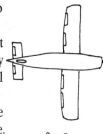

fig. 9

Twirl them around and point them toward the map. See who can get their plane to land closest to an airport. Anyone who actually lands on an airport gets a special prize.

Oriental Ice Cubes.

Every world traveler will want to visit China, but first you have to make sure everyone can use chopsticks.

You can buy chopsticks at toy stores or novelty stores. Or, go out to dinner at a Chinese restaurant and keep the complimentary chopsticks. If you're having many guests at your party, you'll have to go out to dinner several times.

For this game, fill a large bowl with warm water and set it in the middle of the table. Add a couple dozen ice cubes to the water. Give each traveler a pair of chopsticks and a smaller, empty bowl. Have them gather around the bowl of floating ice cubes, and see who can fish out the most ice cubes before they melt. It doesn't matter how they hold the chopsticks—in one hand like a native of China, or with one in each fist—let them use whatever method works to get those ice cubes out.

You might want to mention that it's easiest to catch the ice if they take their time. It only takes a second for the chopstick to melt a "grab hole" in the ice. As soon as this spot is melted, the ice will lift right out.

Give a small prize for every ice cube retrieved, and a larger prize for the overall winner.

Popping Popcorn

If your travelers need more practice with their chopsticks, let them try popped popcorn. This is played in teams of two.

Each pair of travelers gets a bowl of popcorn and an empty bowl. Working together, they must transfer all the popcorn from one bowl to the other, only touching the kernels with the chopsticks. Again, they can hold the chopsticks any way they want. The only rule is that they can't skewer the popcorn! The fastest pair wins, but everyone gets to eat the popcorn.

Origami Puppies

While we're in China, let's skip over to Japan for a chance to make Japanese origami puppies.

For each puppy, start with a square piece of paper and fold it in half to make a triangle. With the longest side of the triangle at the top, fold the side corners down to form the puppy's ears (fig. 10). Fold back the top of the head and the chin, so they're not pointed (fig. 11). Then add a puppy face with markers (fig. 12).

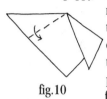

fig.10

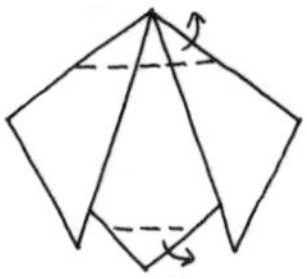

fig. 11

If you don't fold the chin all the way back, it will make a stand for your puppy head. Provide brown, tan, and white paper for different colored puppies. Using brown and black markers, the travelers can make their puppies into beagles or dalmations.

fig. 12

The puppies can keep the travelers company while they enjoy an international meal. For the main course, serve "build your own" Mexican tacos. Give each traveler a couple of taco shells, and set out bowls of ground beef fried with taco seasoning mix, shredded lettuce, diced tomatoes, onions, cheese, and picante sauce.

An International Meal

With it serve hot German potato salad from the delicatessen, French bread, and Chinese fortune cookies. For a special, tropical treat, make Caribbean volcanoes.

Slice the top off an orange and scoop out the insides. Fill the hollow orange with a scoop of orange sherbet, and pour ginger ale over it. Sprinkle crushed orange bits on top.

International Theme Cakes

Finish the meal with an international theme cake made from a round or rectangular cake.

To start off, a rectangular cake makes a great airport runway. Bake the cake in a 9-inch x 13-inch pan as usual, and turn the cake out onto a large platter. Make a runway by frosting the cake with green-tinted icing, except for a strip down the middle covered with chocolate icing.

Add rows of miniature marshmallows for runway lights, red cherries for warning lights, and bits of lemon rind to make dotted lines down the center of the runway. Poke in a plastic plane, with the nose pointing slightly upward, ready for take-off.

A round cake can be transformed into a world with green and blue icing. Frost the cake in blue, and use a toothpick to draw the outline of the continents. If you make a mistake, just spread the frosting flat and try again. Use a decorator tube of green icing to fill in the continents.

Sprinkle brown sugar to make deserts, and add chocolate chips for mountain ranges. Coconut will create polar ice caps, and dabs of leftover blue icing will form inland seas and the Great Lakes.

Prizes from Around the World

It's easy to find prizes to fit an international theme. Almost anything can be related to a country if you're creative.

All zoo animals can correspond to a country, if you think about it long enough. Kangaroos represent Australia, gorillas are African, camels are Arabian, elephants are Indian or Asian, and peacocks come from India. Even domestic animals relate to different countries. There are French bull-dogs, Persian cats, Arabian horses, and Ayrshire cattle from Scotland. Encyclopedias will give you all kinds of information about the origins of many "American" animals.

Any kind of transportation fits your travel theme, like planes, boats, cars, and trains. Sunglasses and sun visors are good for countries near the equator. Anything with hearts, like heart-shaped note pads, heart pins, or heart ponytail holders can represent world unity, the love and acceptance among children of diverse nations.

Edible prizes can come from anywhere, like small bags of Mexican nacho chips, German and French chocolates, and candied Spanish walnuts you can make yourself. Any round candies can represent the world, and bright-colored hard candies and chews give a Spanish fiesta feeling.

This international birthday party will not only provide a good time, but will introduce your travelers to the thrill of learning about other countries. When you combine learning with fun, your guests will have the world by the tail!

15

Back to Nature

There's something about the natural world that attracts people of all ages. Kids love to explore the woods, climb rocks, and poke around in clear-flowing rivers. This wilderness adventure party takes the troops outside. So next time your son or daughter asks, "Can I have a camp-out in the back yard?" your answer can be "Yes!"

Tent Invitations

The only way to truly experience the great outdoors is to spend a night in it, so this party is a sleepover.

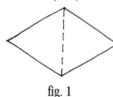

fig. 1

When you make invitations that look like little tents, your guests will know exactly what they're getting into. Cut a diamond shape out of stiff paper

fig. 2

and fold it in half (fig. 1). Turn the folded edge to the left, and cut a slit in the top layer along the right edge (fig. 2).

Fold the tent door open, and glue the right edge strip to the back (fig. 3). Write your message inside the door. You can write on the tent flap, too, since you'll need the space for extra instructions for an overnight party.

fig. 3

Writing on Bark

If you have access to dead wood, you can make bark invitations. One place to get bark is from tree limbs that blow down in heavy winds. If you live near a park or wooded area, get permission to scavenge for bark from fallen trees. Another bark source comes from inside the house. Anyone who burns logs in a fireplace has a constant supply of tree bark.

Birch bark is the easiest to write on, but the smooth inner side of other kinds of bark works, too. Write with a black marker and hand-deliver these natural invitations.

Tents and Campfires

For an outdoor adventure, you won't need to decorate inside the house. But it's important to direct your campers to the back yard when they first arrive. Post a sign by the front walk or near the driveway that says, "Follow the trail to a wilderness adventure." Lay a trail of stones or sticks to lead to the back yard.

The best decorations for this party are the ones growing naturally—trees, bushes, and flowers. Add owls cut from brown paper, and paint their eyes with glow-in-the-dark paint. At dusk, when the campers are occupied with other activities, shine a flashlight over the owls' eyes. They'll come to life with their own light!

If you don't have a tent for your campers, and you don't want to purchase one, rent one. Outfitters and camping stores rent tents at reasonable rates. Check the yellow pages to compare options and prices.

It's tempting to make your own tent with blankets over clotheslines, but that isn't the best idea. A blanket tent is fine for a shady afternoon hideaway, but that's about it. As night falls, mosquitoes and other bugs will infest a blanket tent. And if it rains, homemade tents won't keep your campers dry. You don't want your wilderness explorers retreating to the house in the middle of the night!

The only other thing you need to complete your backyard decor is a grill or fire ring to cook over. If you don't have a charcoal grill, and can't borrow one, you can use a metal trash can to safely have a campfire in your yard. Fill the can with dirt or sand to about twelve inches below the rim. This will make a solid base for your fire.

If you're willing to sacrifice a patch of grass, dig a shallow fire pit in the lawn, clearing the grass around it. Then line the pit with stones. But before you start, check with city ordinances to make sure you won't get in trouble. If these kinds of fires on private property aren't illegal where you live, a ground fire pit makes your camp-out truly authentic.

As your guests arrive, get them settled in the tent. For a mixed crowd, make sure you have one tent for the girls and one for the boys.

Then invite them to a party-starting treat. If you are not sure of your fire-starting skills, use charcoal to get your fire going and light the coals before the campers arrive. If you are a purist, collect tinder and sticks and show your guests how to make a tepee fire. You can even start the blaze with a spark struck from flint and steel.

Give each camper a long, sharpened stick to roast marshmallows. Sandwich the toasted marshmallows between graham crackers and chocolate bars for a classic campfire treat.

Nature Hunt

When your campers are filled with chocolate and marshmallows, send them scavenging for pieces of nature. Give each camper a list of things to find, but don't list the actual objects. Instead write clues, like something sticky, something round, something brown, or something hard. The campers must find a separate object for each clue. For example, a white feather can be used as something soft or something white, but not both. If your back yard isn't very wild or woodsy, add natural items like colorful stones or interesting sticks you've collected elsewhere.

See how creative your campers can be. A dandelion can easily be something yellow, but can also be something white or something wet. Just break the stem to see the milky fluid inside. Give prizes for completed lists and most creative solutions.

Natural Alphabet

The nature hunt will get your campers' brains clicking for this quick-thinking game. The campers sit in a circle and take turns listing things from nature, starting with consecutive letters of the alphabet. The first person might say, "antlers" and the next person "bears," then, "camouflage," "dew," and "evergreen." Each answer must come quickly, without a pause. It's easy at first, but watch out for letters like "Q," "U," and "X." Whenever a person gets stuck on a letter, she is out. Play until one person is left.

Seeing Squares

There are an average of 1,356 living creatures in every square inch of forest topsoil. See how many of them your campers can see in this nature observation game.

Without a microscope, they won't see much in a square inch, so have them search a foot of ground, instead. Use sticks and strings to mark off a square foot of lawn or forest floor. Mark one square for each camper.

Then give each camper a piece of paper and a pencil. With each camper at a different square, give them five minutes to study their square and write down all the different things they see. This includes everything from grass blades to gopher hairs. They probably won't find 1,356 different things, but you'll be surprised how much there is in a square foot of ground, if you take the time to look. Give prizes for the longest lists and the most unique objects.

Which Is Which

Part of appreciating nature is knowing what kinds of plants are growing all around you. This game helps campers learn to identify plants and get to know more about them.

Before the party, collect as many different kinds of leaves as you can find, and use a plant identification field guide to identify them. Tack them to a large piece of cardboard.

Divide the campers into teams, like the Trackers and the Scouts, or the Eagles and the Bears. Be creative with team names. Alternate between teams in guessing the names of each leaf as you point to them. Give one point for each right answer. Everyone on the winning team gets nature prizes.

You can also play "Which is Which?" with different kinds of flowers or berries. Later, some of these same items might show up in your wilderness meal.

Survival Relay

Wilderness survival has four parts: having shelter, fire, water, and food. In this relay race, your campers must see how quickly they can meet their survival needs.

Divide into two teams. The first person on each team must run with a blanket to a clothesline, fence, or other designated object. She drapes the blanket over the object to make her shelter. Then she runs to a pile of sticks and rocks. She arranges the rocks in a circle and the sticks in the center for her fire. Then she dashes to a bucket of water, pours some of the water into a skillet, and throws in a handful of leaves to "cook." She counts to ten, then fishes out the leaves, and dumps out the water.

Since every good camper leaves the landscape just as she found it, the camper must dismantle the fire and retrieve the blanket on the way back to her team. She hands the blanket to the next person, who makes her own tent, fire, and dinner.

The first team that completes the survival training is rewarded for their excellent wilderness skills.

Outdoor Cooking

The birthday meal at a camp out can be the traditional grilled burgers or hot dogs, with roasted corn-on-the-cob, and chips.

Or, go a step further, and cook up dehydrated camping foods. These complete meals come in foil packages and can be purchased at any camping store. You can get anything from spaghetti to apple cobbler. Most meals only require being mixed with boiling water.

Living Off the Land

You can even have a true survivalist meal. Serve only foods that come directly from the land. Spit-cook fresh fish or venison, and serve it with a salad of amaranth, chickweed, and dandelion greens, or other wild plants.

Wild berries add color and flavor to any wilderness meal. For less adventurous campers, strawberries, blueberries, and raspberries fit the bill. Others might like to try more exotic fare like bunchberries, currants, or elderberries.

Natural herb tea is a refreshing treat for a wilderness meal. Some plants that make excellent teas are mint, goldenrod, rose hips, and sassafras.

You will need permission to collect wild edibles from parks and other wild areas, but any park officials will gladly give you any help they can in identifying and finding what you're after. When they find out you're going to help educate people about our natural resources, they might even take you on a personal tour of their wilderness area. But you can still collect wild foods on your own. A good wilderness field guide, like Lee Peterson's *A Field Guide to Wilderness Plants*, or *Tom Brown's Guide to Wild Edible and Medicinal Plants* will give you the information you need. Natural food stores and some grocery stores also sell wild edibles.

You might want to try a combination of the above choices. Serve a "normal" meal with small samples of wild edibles. This way, if your campers don't appreciate dandelion fritters and boiled greenbrier roots, they won't have to eat only cake—especially if the birthday cake is made of honey and acorn flour.

Nature Cakes—Trees and Forests

Whether the birthday cake is made with natural ingredients or not, you can decorate it to fit your wilderness theme. Press green-tinted shredded coconut into the frosting for grass. Then add broccoli bushes  and a river of blue icing. Black jelly beans make good river rocks, and a plastic deer will finish the wilderness scene.

fig. 4

fig. 5

You can make a three-dimensional pine tree cake by cutting a rectangular cake as shown (fig. 4). Lay the small scraps on the top of the cake to make protruding branches. You can arrange the extra cake pieces below the trunk to represent grass, or eat them (fig. 5). Frost the cake in green and poke a few pretzel stick pieces in here and there for branches. Then tuck a couple of small toy birds among the needles.

Camping Gear Prizes

Prizes for a wilderness party should encourage wilderness appreciation. Give small items of camping gear, like pocket knives, compasses, mini-flashlights, camp candles, and folding camp cups. Check your camping store for other ideas.

Campers will love packages of fun camping foods like freeze-dried ice cream and dehydrated french fries. Candy isn't found in nature per se, but it's hard to imagine even a wilderness birthday party without candy prizes. However, try to stick with candy that relates to nature, like animal shaped chocolates, and hard candies made with real fruit juice. Other natural food prizes could include dried fruit, trail mix, and non-refrigerated pudding packs.

Anything with animals on it makes a good prize, like mini-jigsaw puzzles, posters, and postcards. If your guests are real nature buffs, give live plants. Small annuals or cacti are inexpensive and easy to care for.

After all this wilderness exploration, your campers should sleep well. In the morning, the camp-out temporarily moves into the house. Once the campers are dressed and packed, provide a simple breakfast of fruit, doughnuts, and juice. The campers will want to use your bathroom before their parents come to pick them up.

This wilderness birthday gives young people a chance to have fun in the great outdoors, without harming the wilderness.

Religions of the World

Whether your family is Jewish, Hindu, Buddhist, Muslim, Christian, or has other religious beliefs, you can treat your child to a birthday party that will highlight his faith and be great fun. This chapter primarily uses Christianity as an example, but you can use the symbols and popular figures from your own religion just as easily.

Ancient Invitations

Every religion has a body of writings to guide its followers. Model your invitations after these writings to guide your guests to the party.

Fold a piece of stiff paper in half and write "Holy Bible" on the front, or inscribe it to look like the Torah, the Koran, or the Vedas. Inside, write your child's favorite verse or saying on the left, and party information on the right. Use phrases that reflect the style of the religious writing.

A Christian invitation might follow the style of the King James Bible: "And Sally saith unto them: thou shalt not forsake the birthday party which is to come, but shall attendeth on the eighth day of the fourth month of the year of our Lord 1995, at the 242nd house of Green Street. He that heedeth the words of Sally shall receive blessing and honor and have the fun; he that disregardeth this word shall misseth out!"

To go farther back in history, write on a scroll made of rolled paper tied with a ribbon. Or write on paper cut in the traditional tablet shape of the Ten Commandments. For commandment invitations, follow the format of the commands Moses received: "1. Thou shalt have no other plans before

Sally's birthday party. 2.Thou shalt not forsake 242 Green Street on April 8. 3. Thou shalt attend faithfully from 2:00 until 4:00 on that day. 4. Thou shalt have a wonderful time!" You can add more commandments for details about special items to bring or wear.

A Reverent Scene

The poster on your front door can be a witness to your beliefs, as well as a beacon to partyers looking for your house. You can use a generic message like, "Keep the Faith." Or, be bold with something like, "Welcome to Sally's birthday party—a taste of Nirvana!" or, "Christ lives at this party!"

Decorations inside can replicate your place of worship. You can make felt banners using simple patterns (fig. 1), or your place of worship might let you borrow a few of theirs for the day. Candles will add to the atmosphere.

Banner Making

When your guests arrive, they'll notice your bright, colorful banners right off. And they'll love having the opportunity to make their own mini-banners.

Before the party, make a small sample banner so your guests have a

fig. 1

guide to follow. Keep the design simple. Prepare for banner-making by purchasing an assortment of fabric remnants. Cut a 9-inch x 18-inch piece of solid-colored fabric for each guest. Make letter patterns, flower patterns, and hearts out of cardboard.

When your guests arrive, hand out the 9-inch x 18-inch background pieces, and show them your sample. Let them trace letter and shape patterns on whichever color of fabric they want. Felt-tip pens or markers draw well on cloth.

When they cut out the pieces, remind them to cut inside the tracing lines, so they won't show on the finished banner. After they've glued the letters and shapes to the backing piece, demonstrate how to fold the top over a twelve-inch dowel and glue the edge (fig. 2). Then tie a string to each end of the dowel to hang the banner.

banner
back

fig. 2

Making Mates

This game tests knowledge of who's who in religion. Make up related pairs of people. Some examples from the Christian and Jewish tradition would be Abraham and Sarah, Adam and Eve, Samson and Delilah, and Jonah and the whale. Skim through your Bible or other books of worship for more pairs of people, places, and animals.

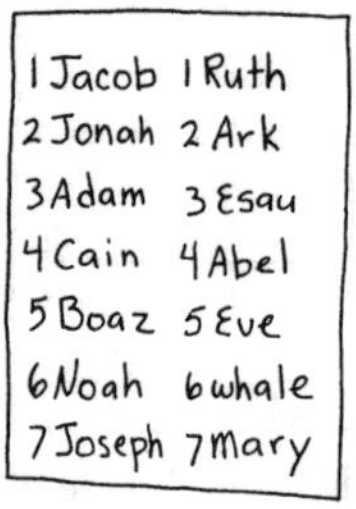

1 Jacob	1 Ruth
2 Jonah	2 Ark
3 Adam	3 Esau
4 Cain	4 Abel
5 Boaz	5 Eve
6 Noah	6 whale
7 Joseph	7 Mary

fig. 3

Divide the pairs into lists, and scramble the pairs (fig. 3). Make copies and give one to each guest. Give a prize to the person who can make the most correct pairs in a set amount of time. How long you allow depends on how many pairs you have and how well the kids know their religious history.

Share and Share Alike

This game is played in pairs and rewards those who can share equally.

Divide the children into pairs. Give the first pair two jars—one empty and one filled with styrofoam pieces. While one person pours the pieces from the full jar into the empty one, the other person watches carefully and calls "Stop!" when it looks like exactly half the pieces have been poured into the second jar. At this, the pourer stops. Count the pieces in each jar to see how close the two players came to dividing the pieces exactly in half, then write down the numbers.

Every pair of players takes a turn trying to divide the styrofoam pieces into two equal portions. After everyone has had a turn, give the best prizes to those who succeeded in sharing alike, and other prizes to those who came close.

Special Bookmarks

To help your guests become more familiar with their worship books, make bookmarks to encourage them to read. Cut small rectangle bookmark shapes from colored poster board. Punch a hole in the top of each bookmark. Provide colored markers and adhesive stickers to decorate with. Loop brightly colored

fig. 4

yarn through the hole in the top. Use two pieces of yarn for each bookmark, and show your guests how to tie a larkshead knot (fig. 4).

Lost Coins

Every religion has stories and parables that can be acted out in games. A good example is the Bible story of the woman who lost a coin and searched the house until she found it. You can find that parable in Luke Chapter 15, starting with verse eight. Read it aloud to your guests, then have them go on their own coin search. Hide pennies, nickels, and dimes around the room, and send them searching. The coins themselves can be prizes, or give prizes for the most pieces of money found, or highest total value of retrieved coins.

I Like Your Nose

All religions teach kindness to others. Give your guests an opportunity to display this by playing a game of compliments.

Have the players sit in a circle with one person in the middle. The person in the middle points to someone and says, "Kathy, I like your nose," and counts to ten. Kathy must say, "Thank you," and think of a compliment to give in return before the person in the center can count to ten. If Kathy can't respond quickly enough, she takes the center spot. The trick is that no one can repeat a compliment someone else has given. Remind people that they don't have to give only physical compliments. They can also say nice things about people's personalities.

Food of Your Faith

After everyone's spirits have been fed with wonderful compliments, it's time to feed their stomachs.

Serve foods that can be found in the lands where well-known religious figures once lived, or foods that appear in your religion's teachings. At a Christian party, serve items native to the Holy Land, like dates and nuts. Serve unleavened bread (or crackers) to commemorate Passover, and grape juice to symbolize wine. Fish and lamb are also foods associated with the Bible.

Use an international cookbook for authentic lamb and fish recipes, and for more menu ideas. A little research in religious writings will give you all sorts of ideas for religion-related foods. This birthday meal can give your guests a chance to try new foods, while they learn about religious traditions.

Heart Cake

Let the birthday cake reflect the love all religions promote. Frost your cake with white and decorate it with heart-shaped candies and heart-shaped sugar cookie cutouts.

Or, make a heart cake. Mix the cake according to package directions, then bake it in one round eight-inch pan and one square eight-inch pan. After the cake is cool, cut the round layer in half and place it on the sides of the square layer (fig. 5). Frost with red, white, or pink icing, and decorate it with colorful borders of small heart candies and other candy pieces.

fig. 5

Loving Favors

Give prizes that will help your guests become more attuned to their faith. Pocket copies of religious texts are good, or small plaques and buttons with religious sayings. Plastic animals from religious stories are fun and inexpensive.

Get ideas for food prizes by reviewing stories from your faith. Using our Bible example, there are chocolate candy coins (widow's mite in Luke, chapter 21), apples (Garden of Eden in Genesis, chapter 3), gummi worms (Moses' rod becomes a serpent in Exodus, chapter 13), chocolate graham crackers (manna in the wilderness in Exodus chapter 13), candy corn (parable of the sower in Matthew, chapter 13), and fish crackers (fishers of men in Matthew, chapter 4).

Toy models that correspond to stories make good bigger prizes, like a model boat to represent Noah's ark, and scented candles like the incense in the tabernacle. Use your imagination to invent all kinds of fun prizes that are also inspirational.

A faith-filled party makes a unique birthday no one can duplicate. As you incorporate your own favorite stories of Buddha, Christ, Mohammed, or Yaweh, your party will become an enlightening experience your child will never forget.

PART FIVE

On the Road

Planning a party takes more than great ideas and craft supplies. It also requires contingency plans and organization. You can't anticipate everything that will happen when you mix children, games, and food, but you can head trouble off with a little forethought.

Here's how to avoid difficult situations and keep your wonderful plans working wonderfully!

I'm Just Not Good at Planning, And Besides, My House...

What if your child's best friend is allergic to your cat? Or what if your kitchen is going to be torn up by remodelers for the next two months? Or you simply don't have the time or energy to make decorations, collect craft materials, or organize games?

Take the party on the road.

A glance through the newspaper, a quick perusal through the yellow pages, or a phone call to the local Chamber of Commerce will yield an abundance of ideas for a party away from home.

A Zoo Party

On a sunny day, load the kids in the car and head for the zoo. Invitations for a zoo party can follow the ideas suggested for the jungle party, since a zoo is really a slice of jungle life. Because animal watching is the prime entertainment, you don't need to plan games. Just have a bag of goodies and one nice party favor to give each child as a "thanks-for-coming" gift. Check chapter eight, the jungle chapter, for party gift ideas.

Most zoos have picnic areas where you can celebrate with cake and presents. Check ahead of time. If they don't you can always go to a restaurant. Just be sure to make reservations beforehand, in a private room, if possible. And make it clear you'll be bringing your own cake. Purchase drinks and appetizers, and tip generously.

Checking Out the Museum

If the day is rainy or cold, go to a museum instead of the zoo. At a museum of natural history, children can still see animals—stuffed ones that won't bite their fingers. For those who are more science-minded, or would like a space adventure party, try a planetarium, or science museum. As with the zoo party, no planned games are needed, but a parting gift is a must.

Most zoos, museums, and other tourist attractions have gift shops and novelty stores. You can make sure your parting gifts are exactly what each child wants by letting them choose their own gifts. Set a dollar limit to keep them from bankrupting you, and a time limit to keep them from driving the clerk crazy.

Off to a Ball Game

For those who want a little more action on their birthday outing, go to a ball game. Use the invitations from chapter 10, "Play Ball." You don't need to pay top dollar to see a professional team. Most kids are just as happy at a college or high school game. But you will have to spend a little more on food. What fun is a baseball or football game without hot dogs and drinks? Purchase pennants or other souvenirs for each child to take home.

After the game, the park officials won't appreciate having you eat cake in the stands. You could have a tailgate party in the parking lot, or move that part of the party elsewhere, like a park or restaurant.

fig. 1

Movies and Theater

Movie matinees and community theater make fun, no-fuss parties. Invitations can look like an admission ticket (fig. 1), or like a theater program (fig. 2).

fig. 2

As with the ball game, purchase treats at the show, and celebrate with the cake and presents at another location.

Picnics and Hikes

You can use a variation of the wilderness party by going on a hike or a picnic. Use bark invitations, or invitations written on ant-shaped paper cutouts with legs made of pipe cleaners (fig. 3). Not that there will be any ants at *your* picnic!

The main entertainment at a picnic party is exploring. Find a park with good hiking trails, walking paths, and water. Water is a must, since everyone loves to poke around in a bubbly stream, skip rocks over a still pond, and throw bread crumbs to the ducks.

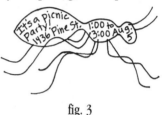

fig. 3

The key to a successful picnic party is good supervision. If possible, have one adult for every three children, and make sure you know where the kids are at all times. If there are rangers or other park personnel around, tell them who you are, how many are in your group, and how long you plan to stay. It never hurts to have a few more eyes on the lookout for potential trouble.

A Trip to the Farm

If your party guests are used to city life, a trip to a farm is a real treat. If you know anyone who farms, ask if you can spend an afternoon at their place. Some kids have never seen a cow up close, and would be tickled by a chance to try milking one. Other farm attractions include feeding chickens, petting piglets, rubbing a woolly sheep, and maybe even riding on a horse.

A variation of this is to visit a fruit farm, like an apple orchard or a U-Pick strawberry farm. These places offer a variety of foods and food samples, and may let you celebrate with cake and presents on the premises.

All these outings, plus others you come up with, eliminate your home from the party scene. They provide unique opportunities to entertain without disturbing your spouse, if he or she works nights and sleeps days, or the construction crew who promised the job would be finished last week!

CONCLUSION

Can I Do This on My Budget? And Other Practical Matters

The secret to keeping party costs under control is to plan ahead. The sooner you know what type of party you want, the sooner you can start looking for sales on the things you'll need.

Visiting those Garage Sales

The best place to get good stuff cheap is at garage sales or yard sales. You never know what kind of interesting things you'll find—everything from stacks of used coloring books to bags of clothespins and tiny army men, and all kinds of clothes.

When going to garage sales, keep your mind open to new ideas. You might not be caught dead in that calf-length, pea-green skirt, but cut into thin strips, it will make fine jungle vines. Or, maybe you were going to make Morse code invitations for a mystery party, but when you saw that sack of magazines for fifty cents, letter-cutout invitations suddenly seemed like a better idea.

Don't keep your party a secret. You'll be amazed at how many people have stuff they are glad to lend you, or give away, if they know you're interested.

Sale Shopping

Become a sales scavenger. Almost everything goes on sale sooner or later. The sooner you start watching for clearance sales on paper products, fabrics, favors, and foods, the more likely you are to catch those sales.

Saving and Storage

And save everything. Try to carve out a spot somewhere in your house to store items you're saving for future parties. It can be a closet shelf, a drawer, or a space under the bed. Stash paper towel rolls, old magazines, and other valuable "trash" in your party spot. When it's time to decorate and create, everything will be at hand.

Lists Are the Key

To be completely organized, keep two lists of your party stuff. One is a list of things you have, and the other is a list of things you're looking for. Take the "looking for" list with you everywhere you go. Then, when you impulsively stop at a garage sale, or see a special on paper plates at the grocery store, you can check your list to see what you need.

Keep the "have" list in your storage space. Every time you stash away your latest find, whether it was on your "looking for" list or is simply an item that might turn out useful, write it on your "have" list. This way you'll always know what's in your storage space without having to dig through it.

Until Next Year

Use this same space to store party remnants after the party is over. Of course, you'll give away decorations the guests want to take home, but much of the rest can be saved. Roll streamers to use again, save animal cutouts that can be used for more than one theme, and keep odd pieces of construction paper, yarn, or ribbon.

With this kind of organization, your parties will be wonderful for your child, and painless for you. When the time comes, pick out your child's favorite theme, put on your creative thinking hat, and create a one-of-a-kind party everyone will love!

Games Index

Index

About the Author

Jane Chase lives in St. Paul, Minnesota with her husband Richard, their cat Alpha, and two black-and-white rats, Gertrude and Camile. She likes canoeing and camping, and is interested in wilderness lore and tracking. Other hobbies include reading and working jigsaw puzzles.

Jane has been published in a variety of Christian and secular magazines, and is a regular contributor to *Guide*. She is also a professional artist as well as a baker for Marriott Corporation. Her work with children includes serving as Art Director at Covenant Pines Bible Camp, and Children's Ministry Director's assistant at Lima Rescue Home in Ohio.

Available from Brighton Publications, Inc.

Romantic At-Home Dinners: Sneaky Strategies for Couples with Kids by Nan Booth/Gary Fischler

Kid-Tastic Birthday Parties: The Complete Party Planner for Today's Kids by Jane Chase

Games for Baby Shower Fun by Sharon Dlugosch

Baby Shower Fun by Sharon Dlugosch

Reunions for Fun-Loving Families by Nancy Funke Bagley

An Anniversary to Remember: Years One to Seventy-Five by Cynthia Lueck Sowden

Folding Table Napkins: A New Look at a Traditional Craft by Sharon Dlugosch

Table Setting Guide by Sharon Dlugosch

Tabletop Vignettes by Sharon Dlugosch

Games for Wedding Shower Fun by Sharon Dlugosch, Florence Nelson

Wedding Plans: 50 Unique Themes for the Wedding of Your Dreams by Sharon Dlugosch

Wedding Hints & Reminders by Sharon Dlugosch

Wedding Occasions: 101 New Party Themes for Wedding Showers, Rehearsal Dinners, Engagement Parties, and More! by Cynthia Lueck Sowden

Dream Weddings Do Come True: How to Plan a Stress-free Wedding by Cynthia Kreuger

Don't Slurp Your Soup: A Basic Guide to Business Etiquette by Betty Craig

Meeting Room Games: Getting Things Done in Committees by Nan Booth

Hit the Ground Running: Communicate Your Way to Business Success by Cynthia Kreuger

These books are available in selected stores and catalogs. If you're having trouble finding them in your area, send a self-addressed, stamped, business-size envelope and request ordering information from:

Brighton Publications, Inc.
P.O. Box 120706
St. Paul, MN 55112-0706

or call: 1-800-536-BOOK